LIFE AND MORALS

THE MACMILLAN COMPANY
NEW YORK · BOSTON · CHICAGO · DALLAS
ATLANTA · SAN FRANCISCO

MACMILLAN AND CO., Limited
LONDON · BOMBAY · CALCUTTA · MADRAS
MELBOURNE

THE MACMILLAN COMPANY
OF CANADA, Limited
TORONTO

LIFE
and MORALS

by S. J. Holmes

NEW YORK   1948

THE MACMILLAN COMPANY

Copyright, 1948, by
S. J. HOLMES

All rights reserved—no part of this book may be reproduced in any form without permission in writing from the publisher, except by a reviewer who wishes to quote brief passages in connection with a review written for inclusion in magazine or newspaper.

First Printing.

PRINTED IN THE UNITED STATES OF AMERICA

Preface

IN THE PRESENT VOLUME morals have been treated from a naturalistic viewpoint in the determination of which biological concepts have inevitably played an important part. For this reason I had thought of entitling it *The Biological Outlook on Morals,* but since frequent references are made to psychological factors and social forces, the term "biological" would have to be construed in a sense that might be deemed too inclusive to be appropriate, especially when employed by a biologist. Hence after much futile effort to find a better title, I finally decided upon *Life and Morals,* which does not altogether please me, although, so far as it goes, it truly designates what the book is about. After all, life is very much the same sort of thing fundamentally, whether it is manifested in the behavior of cells, the instincts of animals, or the moral conduct of men.

It is, as I have attempted to show, highly advantageous in many ways to look upon morals as a purely natural product, a form of life intimately associated in nature and origin with other forms of living. This outlook on morals has the advantage of affording a basis for a scientific interpretation of its subject matter. Traditionally morals have long been concerned to no small degree with the relations of man to existences beyond his actual world—to gods, and other supernatural beings, to occult powers more or less amenable to control by magic, and to a future life for which it is important to make the right kind of preparation. Morality is still widely held to have its closest relations with theology and metaphysics. Probably the most important trend in its history is its gradual transfer of filiation from these disciplines to the biological, psychological and social sciences.

According to the famous generalization of Auguste Comte, man's interpretations of his world pass through three stages: (1) the theological, in which phenomena are attributed to the activities of supernatural beings; (2) the metaphysical, in which supernatural beings are replaced by abstract principles; and (3) the positive, when the aim is to ascertain the laws to which observed phenomena conform. In the main, ethics has followed this course in its development, but to a greater extent than most fields of knowledge it is now in all three stages at the same time. Very diverse opinions prevail as to the nature of right and wrong, the theological grounds, if any, of moral obligation; the authority of conscience, and especially the methods to be employed in the solution of moral problems. Ethics is still in a stage which most other disciplines have largely passed through. The situation is productive, not only of much confusion in the popular mind, but of many sharply opposed attitudes on matters of moral practice. In a later chapter I have attempted to show that a number of good causes find their most serious obstacle in an ethics based on authority. Such an ethics tends by nature to be resistant to change and hence to become less well adapted to a changing world.

There is, I believe, no way out of the present chaos and confusion except through the adoption of a scientifically grounded ethics. We need the same kind of understanding of the phenomena of the moral life that we aim to have of life on the biological level. All branches of science have their practical applications, and these increase in effectiveness with the increase of our theoretical insight and understanding.

Morality is, *par excellence,* concerned with practice. It is, of course, not restricted to the narrow realm of acts that can be catalogued in a code. Obviously many activities are morally indifferent, but any act that has an important effect upon human welfare acquires moral significance. Hence we require all the knowledge we can obtain in order to keep us from continually doing the wrong things with the very best of intentions. A scientific ethics, therefore, emphasizes the essential relation between wisdom and virtue which was so much stressed by the ancient Greeks and which for many centuries thereafter failed to obtain adequate recognition on account of the dominant influence of an ethics based on authority. Ethics is not an isolated field of knowledge, and the effect of restricting its sphere of application is to promote its sterility of which a number of writers have complained. It makes use of all kinds of knowledge that can aid in the realization of its aims, but its fundamental problems, both theoretical and practical, are especially concerned with knowledge of the nature of man, his springs of conduct, and the biological, cultural, economic, religious, and other forces which have made him what he is.

My chief aim in this volume is to present an outlook on morals from the standpoint of the life sciences. Accordingly, I have emphasized the importance of the organic viewpoint. Moral conduct in human society is viewed as having much the same functional significance as the cooperative behavior of the parts of the body in maintaining the life of the whole. In the adjustment of their egoistic and altruistic activities, these parts have to do quite precisely the right things, else they and their associates will quickly come to grief. Much the same relations obtain in a hive of bees and to a less degree in other social groups. The life of a human society also depends on the proper conduct of individuals in their several rôles; at least, the behavior of individuals cannot be too antisocial or chaos, if not destruction, will soon result. These similar relationships are not mere analogies. They depend upon the basic properties of life; and our own morality is all of a piece with the integrative behavior on other levels which is required for carrying on the enterprise of living. Human nature has been molded, not only for self-preservation, but for the perpetuation of group life. So have our cells. The view that morality is an integral part of the life-preserving and life-perpetuating activities at all levels has far-reaching implications both theoretical and practical. It was first brought into prominence through the doctrine of organic evolution and it has influenced opinions on moral standards, the grounds of moral obligation, the nature and authority of conscience, the significance of our native human traits, the relation of egoism and altruism, and various other long-standing matters of controversy. It affords the possibility of a comprehensive and unified conception of the field, bringing it into closer and more helpful relations with other branches of knowledge, and emphasizing the importance of employing scientific methods in the solution of its problems. If such an outlook contributes to a scientific understanding of the why's and wherefore's of human conduct and the influences whereby conduct can be improved, it cannot be valued too highly. It would have much the same *kind* of beneficent effect that insight into the causes of disease and the mode of operation of remedies have had upon the practical art of healing our bodily and mental ills. Our present remoteness from this goal has recently been remarked upon by Professor John Dewey, whose hostility to "antinaturalism" seems to have been increasing with his years, in his statement that "in social and moral matters we are twenty-five hundred years behind the discovery of Hippocrates as to the natural quality of the causes of disease and health and behind his dictum that all events are equally sacred and equally natural."

The people of the world face many grave problems of conduct for which no ready-made solutions are available. Like the physician, we must understand the nature and causes of the ills we hope to overcome if we would discover the remedies that would effect their cure. Among the more disturbing problems which have forced themselves upon our attention as never before, and which will demand a still larger share of our attention in the years to come, are those presented by the moral behavior of groups. A few of the later chapters of this volume will deal with some of these problems. The distinctive character of group morals, in so far as they differ from the morals of individual life, is, to a large extent, the natural outgrowth of the methods by which biological and social evolution have been effected. In dealing with them the insights made possible by the development of the life sciences can scarcely fail to be of great value.

In the preparation of the present volume I have profited by the criticisms of Professors G. P. Adams and S. C. Pepper, Department of Philosophy, University of California, and my former colleagues in the same university, Dr. Chauncey Leake and Dr. H. B. Torrey. To Dr. R. H. Lowie I am indebted for reading the first nine chapters, including those lying within the field of cultural anthropology, and I have submitted to Dr. George Stratton the discussions in chapters IV to VII dealing largely with matters of psychology. The manuscript of the whole volume has been read critically by my wife to whom I owe the elimination of a number of infelicities of expression. I cannot be sure that I have not fallen into a number of errors of fact or interpretation, but my apprehensions on this score have been sensibly allayed by the qualified critics who have been kind enough to peruse my manuscript. I am quite sure that my conclusions will meet with opposition from a considerable proportion of my readers because I have attacked a number of doctrines which are widely held.

The first three pages of the chapter on "The Ethics of Enmity" were first published in an article of this title in *The American Naturalist* whose editor has kindly permitted me to reproduce them here.

UNIVERSITY OF CALIFORNIA, BERKELEY

Contents

Preface		v
I.	The Moral Behavior of Cells	1
II.	Naturalism and Supernaturalism in Ethics	5
III.	Conflicting Moral Standards and Theories	17
IV.	Natural Selection and the Evolution of Morals	50
V.	Evolutionary Theories of Conscience	56
VI.	Human Nature in the Light of Darwinism	71
VII.	The Deep Roots of Altruism	102
VIII.	The Moral Savage	116
IX.	Religion the Handmaid of Morals	130
X.	Some Controverted Questions of Right and Wrong	144
	Divorce	148
	Birth Control	153
	Euthanasia	159
	The Opposition to Animal Experimentation	162
	The Ethics of Belief	165
XI.	The Ethics of Enmity	176
XII.	The Justification of War	191
XIII.	Our Expanding Moral Horizon	202
Appendix—Bibliographical References and Comments		214
Index		227

CHAPTER I

The Moral Behavior of Cells

> Organization in an individual creature is made possible only by dependence of each part on all, and of all on each. This is also true of social organization.
> —HERBERT SPENCER, *The Study of Sociology*

> Moral procedure, then, differs from life in its more elementary form, through the fact that interests are organized. Morality is only life where this has assumed the form of the forward movement of character, nationality, and humanity.
> —R. B. PERRY, *The Moral Economy*

THE MORAL BEHAVIOR of cells! What an idea! But I hasten to explain that I am now speaking of behavior from a purely objective standpoint, as it would be contemplated by a behaviorist. Cells act in many ways that conduce to the welfare of other cells. Ordinarily they are very well behaved. Occasionally they misbehave, as in the case of cancer cells which become insubordinate and antagonistic to the extent of destroying the organisms of which they form a part. Viewed just as behavior, the activities of cells are closely analogous to those of human beings in an organized society. People whose conduct affects their group much as cancer cells affect the body are justly condemned as highly immoral. I am, of course, making an outrageous extension of the commonly accepted meaning of the term "moral." But for a particular purpose there is at times some justification in following the procedure of Humpty Dumpty, who said to Alice: "When *I* use a word it means just what I choose it to mean—neither more nor less." I avail myself of this privilege all the more readily because ethics has traditionally been closely associated with philosophy, and philosophers are notoriously prone to develop vocabularies of their own in order to expound their distinctive views.

The volume with which I was occupied immediately preceding the present one dealt with the basic biological problem of organic form. Although this topic is apparently remote from the subject considered here, and in many respects undoubtedly is so, there are nevertheless certain similarities growing out of the fact that both deal with the integration of life processes. Both are concerned with the kinds of behavior conducive to harmonious living. Both deal with egoistic and altruistic actions and their effects upon the life of the whole. Both face the problem of how cooperating individualities—whether cells or human beings—came to be so constituted that they tend to work together, with greater or less degrees of success, to maintain the life of the whole of which they are parts.

The development of any highly organized creature is absolutely dependent upon the precise coordination of a great multitude of cellular reactions. Deviations from normal procedures constantly occur, and sometimes lead to unfortunate results. But for the most part, instead of leading to further departures from the normal path of development, they are corrected by a sort of *vis medicatrix naturae*. These automatic regulatory activities are manifested not only in development and regeneration but in the continued adjustment of functions in the adult individual. In all higher organisms life is ever dependent upon the behavior of cells which do not live for themselves alone. They supply the needs of other cells upon whose functioning they are themselves dependent.

Every organized body is the seat of innumerable altruistic activities which at times may lead to the sacrifice of individual units. In early development a cell may play one or another of a number of rôles. Cells of a frog's blastula may become nerve cells, a part of the lens of the eye, or cells of the outer epidermis of the skin, according to the region into which they are grafted. What a cell becomes before it acquires an irretrievable fixity or set depends upon its relations to surrounding parts. It is these environmental influences that determine which of its many possibilities of differentiation are realized. The progress of experimental embryology has shown that differentiation is essentially epigenetic—a result of interaction—but it rests upon a basis of preformation represented by the outfit of genes with which every cell is provided.

Development has come to be looked upon more and more as a series of responses to an ever-changing complex of stimuli. The nature of the response depends upon the genes which are awakened to activity in a particular cellular environment in which they can play their specific rôles as the drama of development unfolds.

As an achievement in cooperative activity, the development of an individual can scarcely be paralleled by any of the products of human effort. Orderly development which depends upon gene activity at the right places and at the right times naturally requires a highly specific outfit of genetic factors to start with. How the genes came to be fitted for their respective rôles is an evolutionary problem which the Darwinian would explain in terms of selection. Most gene mutations are bad, and many of them lead to fatal effects. Occasionally there are beneficial mutations and the evolutionist may interpret the complex of genes with their fitting reaction modes as the outcome of successive survivals during the long course of phylogenetic history. We may assume that cells have been fitted for cooperative behavior much as the members of an insect society have been fitted for their several rôles in the communal life.

Viewing development as essentially a series of responses to stimuli, we may conclude that natural selection has busied itself chiefly in picking up favorable reaction modes which lead to the formation of her varied types of viable organisms. In an essentially similar manner Nature has fitted animals for social life, and she has made some progress in this direction with man. Human beings never have made and probably never will make nearly as good a job of cooperative living as is exhibited by the components of the individual organism. Our own species is much less socialized than many kinds of social insects. Nevertheless, social groups, whether of cells or loose aggregates of human nomads, have much the same biological significance. They are mutual benefit associations and are dependent upon a measure of activity which is altruistic in effect, whether or not it is consciously so in intent.

After all, life wherever found, is engaged in playing much the same game. One of the first adequately to take in this great fact in its far-reaching implications was Herbert Spencer, who elaborated it throughout the range of his *Synthetic Philosophy* from *First Principles* to his *Principles of Ethics*. This fruitful conception formed an inspiring theme which appealed with especial force to Spencer's strong generalizing bent. For Spencer moral life is not something *sui generis,* but an outgrowth of life in its simpler phases with which it always remains fundamentally akin and which, quite as much as these phases, is an inevitable product of the evolutionary process. Both Darwin and Spencer endeavored to give a purely naturalistic account of the nature and evolution of morals, but their approach to the subject was from different directions and resulted in viewpoints in part mutually supporting and in part divergent, as will be more specifically described in a later chapter.

CHAPTER II

Naturalism and Supernaturalism in Ethics

> The enormous rôle played in popular morals by appeal to the supernatural and the quasi-magical is in effect a desperate admission of the futility of our science.
> —JOHN DEWEY, *Human Nature and Conduct*

THE CONCEPTION OF MORAL behavior as a derivative of life activities on a more primitive level afforded a new outlook which could not fail to have an important influence on moral theory. The advancement of science and especially the establishment of the principle of organic evolution has enabled us to interpret that phase of our vital activities which falls within the category of moral behavior in an eminently natural and sensible manner. We can look upon the whole field of morals as a perfectly natural development without recourse to supernaturalism, or appeals to "principles that transcend experience" to any greater extent than we are justified in so doing in dealing with the phenomena of physiology or historical geology. As a theoretical viewpoint evolutionary naturalism applied to morals has been very much in evidence for quite a few decades. Unlike the doctrine of evolution in biology it is still in the controversial stage among qualified scholars. In the following chapters the attempt will be made to show that the viewpoint here adopted has the merit of giving us a broader outlook on the field, a more scientific knowledge of the phenomena of the moral life, and that in accordance with the principle that better understanding leads to more effective practice, it will aid us in solving aright the moral problems with which we are confronted. This viewpoint still arouses much the same kind of alarm that was called forth by the doctrine of evolution and various other scientific generalizations that were deemed inconsistent with widespread beliefs.

One of the foremost matters of concern in the controversial period inaugurated by Darwin's *Origin of Species* was how morals would be affected by the new doctrine. To this question many of Darwin's contemporaries had their answer ready. Morality would simply go to the dogs, or at least to the apes. If we came from brutes, it was alleged, and the fact became generally known, we would naturally act like brutes. Believing that man was created in the image of God and that he owed what goodness he might possess to his divine origin, the people of the mid-Victorian period were deeply shocked when Darwin propounded views so strikingly at variance with their traditional ideology. The theory that man is the product of natural forces and that his intellect, his moral impulses, and the emotional basis of his religious life, have been evolved as the outcome of the struggle for existence, was regarded as subversive of the very foundations of morality and religion. The violent attacks that greeted the *Origin of Species* and *The Descent of Man* were inspired far less by the purely biological aspects of Darwin's views than by their presumably destructive effect on beliefs upon which the stability of society was held to depend.

The more spectacular battles over evolution are now matters of history, but after the doctrine of man's descent from lower animals was accepted, not only by scientists, but by philosophers, moralists, liberal-minded theologians, and educated people generally, opposition to a purely naturalistic ethics continued to be rife. Supernaturalism in one form or another still figures in many of the treatises on ethics used in our colleges and universities. Evolution is usually conceded to have its applications in ethics as in the biological and social sciences, but the deeper problems of morals are held to belong to metaphysics and to be untouched by whatever happens in the realm of mere things. Hence many writers on ethics are loath to concede that the doctrine of evolution has affected the proud position of their science in any fundamental way. The English philosopher, Benn, tells us, "The doctrine of evolution from which so much had been hoped throws no fresh light on the problems of ethics." Those who base ethics on metaphysical principles which transcend all natural events are willingly persuaded that evolution carries no threat to the security of their position. W. R. Sorley, for instance, stated in his able discussion, *On the Ethics of Naturalism,* that, "however valuable may be the information we get from experience, as to the gradual evolution of conduct, its nature and end can only be explained by a principle that transcends experience."

Not a few metaphysicians have attempted to show that, starting with the facts of moral experience, one is led by an inexorable logic to the adoption of the fundamental tenets of theology. Being a mere biologist, unskilled in the employment of philosophical dialectics, I shall not attempt to controvert this claim. And I shall, in general, avoid becoming entangled in the discussions of basic metaphysical problems which bulk so large in the literature on ethics. At least I shall try. Perhaps it might be pointed out to me that whatever opinions I may be led to express have logical implications which, if rigorously pursued, would force me into this or that metaphysical camp, and might even land me in the lap of the Church of England along with a goodly number of scholarly Oxonians. I concede this possibility and am duly impressed by it. Humbly conceding that the fault may be mine, I must confess that the perusal of a number of attempts to deduce philosophical and theological conclusions from the facts of moral behavior leaves me unconvinced.

The long-standing strife between a naturalistic and a supernaturalistic interpretation of the world is still with us, but it has shifted its ground. The old natural theology of Paley and the Bridgewater Treatises which endeavored to derive its chief support from the phenomena of the material world has to a large extent been superseded by other forms based upon the facts of the inner life. The outer world with its vipers, blood flukes and epidemic diseases proved to be a rather thorny domain for the older forms of the design argument and it has been largely abandoned by the more critically minded. The newer natural theology, like the old, derives much of its support from a lot of things which, it is alleged, science cannot explain, and which necessitate, in one way or another, an appeal to God. It concedes that the universe is a rational order in which miracles in the crude sense of violation of the course of nature do not occur. At the same time it derives much satisfaction from the gaps and discontinuities in our world of phenomena. It makes much of the difficulties of explaining the origin of life, the emergence of mind, and especially the existence in man of the power of recognizing moral values. Upon this latter foundation a number of moral philosophers have endeavored to found a whole system of theology. The effort to show that the logical implications of the moral life inevitably lead to the establishment of the existence and goodness of God forms the dominant motive of many of the books on ethics that have appeared during the last half century. This general thesis is supported by much elaborate and profound argumentation. It forms the common theme of the volumes of the Gifford Lectures, the authors of which are virtually committed *ipso facto* to a defense of this doctrine. W. R. Sorley, for instance, in his lectures on *Moral Values and the Idea of God* stated, "the recognition of the moral order and of its relation to nature and man involves the acknowledgment of the Supreme Mind, or God, as the ground of all reality."

In his Gifford Lectures on *The Faith of a Moralist*, Professor A. E. Taylor contends that "the good man who thinks out to the end the implications of his loyalty to the moral good ... is committed to a belief in the final coincidence of the 'ought' and the 'is' in virtue of their common source in a transcendent living and personal Good—one, complete, eternal—the only belief which rightfully deserves to be called belief in God," and further that "the moral life of man, rightly studied, bears impressive testimony to three great strictly *supernatural* or *other-world* realities—God, grace, eternal life." And A. J. Balfour, who long devoted his literary talents and dialectical skill to exposing the unsoundness of the metaphysical foundations of what he calls naturalism, contended (by way of clearing ground for the establishment of a firm foundation of religious belief), "Theism of a religious type is necessary if the great values on which depend all our higher life are to be reasonably sustained." I might cite further Professor James Ward, who, like Balfour, long waged war against his favorite *bête noire* of "naturalism" and expressed much the same viewpoint as to the implications of moral values.

The derivation of conclusions concerning the nature of God from the moral experience of man is an enterprise fraught with possibilities of many a slip between the data and the final deductions. That the enterprise can be successfully carried out so as to compel the assent of everyone with sufficient philosophical insight to follow the argument, is a question with which I am not here concerned. But, having to the best of my ability followed through a number of such efforts involving much subtle philosophizing and many hair-splitting distinctions, I have acquired a lively impression of the perils of the task. And when we look upon man as an animal a bit more advanced than the rest, a product of the evolutionary process which has molded his native intelligence and emotional endowments as it has fashioned his bodily form to meet the exigencies of survival, the difficulties of the task appear to be considerably augmented.

The volumes of Gifford Lectures to which I have alluded are typical of numerous other treatises on ethics from the standpoint of the newer natural theology. In a series of these lectures, somewhat out of the usual line in that it is devoted to the "domain of natural science," the prominent English physicist Professor E. W. Hobson has remarked, "Theism is now very frequently regarded as finding its main support in the existence of the domain of moral standards, whereas, in much of the thought of the eighteenth century, and even later, this relation of dependence was taken in the reverse order." The design argument of Paley *et al.* is regarded as no longer defensible. Although purposiveness, of a kind, may be exhibited in the activities of a living organism it is a "long step to pass on to a unitary purposiveness associated with all natural phenomena." Apparently Professor Hobson is not very enthusiastic over the support for theology furnished by the domain of natural science: "The argument in favor of Theism . . . generally regarded as the most important and convincing is the Moral Argument which is based upon the human conception of moral values," but he leaves this aspect of the problem as outside the scope of the topic he had chosen to treat.

A similar restriction of subject matter is exhibited in the closely reasoned series of Gifford Lectures by W. D. Ross on *The Foundations of Ethics,* which is largely devoted, like his previous treatise on *The Right and the Good,* to an analysis of what we mean by the right and the good, and a detailed critical analysis of the various theories about them. No elaborate arguments are developed with the aim of deducing theological conclusions from the facts of the moral life, but after paying an appropriate tribute to the broad and generous provision with which Lord Gifford established his bequest, Dr. Ross in his final paragraph points out that the establishment of ethics on a firm and rational foundation "is a necessary preliminary to any natural theology which is going to ascribe any moral attributes to God."

Apparently it was the fact that writers on ethics have long shown a conspicuous tendency to indulge in elaborate and frequently tedious dialectical argumentation over metaphysical problems, which elicited the remark of F. C. S. Schiller, who shares with William James and Santayana a refreshing ebullience and insubordination, that "ethics is a dead tradition which has very little relation to the actual facts of moral sentiment." * Ethics has been set off sharply from other branches of knowledge in the effort to keep it tied securely to the apron strings of metaphysics and theology. The fear has long prevailed that unless ethics is so tied its influence on human conduct will be sadly impaired. In a very recent volume on *The Modern Theory of Evolutionary Naturalism,* Dr. Quillian expresses deep concern over the prospect that if the doctrines of the new evolutionary naturalism were correct, "there would be no moral judgments and no choice. ... there would be no consciousness of obligation, no awareness of what I ought to be but am not." The conviction is more or less prevalent that those whose moral con-

---

* A somewhat similar verdict has been expressed by Mr. Havelock Ellis: "No man has ever counted the books that have been written about morals. . . . Yet it can scarcely be that on any subject are the books that have been written more unprofitable, one might even say unnecessary."

duct is not grounded on theological sanctions should be reminded, in all kindness and delicacy, that they can be passably decent only at the sacrifice of consistency.

The dread specter of the naturalistic explainer continues to haunt some of our professional philosophers, to say nothing of less sophisticated souls. This fear is the lineal descendant of the old opposition to the encroachments of science in the realm of nature, but is it any better grounded than its predecessor? The various branches of science as they advance, and especially as a better understanding of their basic problems is reached, draw more closely and helpfully together. The extension of naturalistic explanation is not limited to matters of theoretical understanding, but results in practical applications of the greatest value, as is so conspicuously illustrated in the progress of medicine. The notion that naturalistic explanation is a menace to the preservation of our moral values has a tendency to convert ethics into a relatively sterile discipline. Instead of aiding the cause of good morals, it tends to produce the reverse effect by depriving ethics of the kind of insights and understanding that has contributed so potently to the beneficent influence of other fields of knowledge.

No enlightened ethicist denies that scientific knowledge is often very helpful in enabling us to attain good ends. But many of them contend that on the really basic problems of ethics science has nothing to say. They would relegate science to a purely subordinate and ancillary rôle. One finds all grades of appreciation, as well as condescending acknowledgment of the service of science, in the solution of moral problems. Many benighted individuals look upon the utility of science as limited to supplying our material needs; in its wider bearings they regard it with a vague dread or even with positive hostility. Such attitudes tend to exclude the application of science from those fields in which it can perform its greatest service. Like all practical disciplines, ethics must employ scientific methods to achieve its ends. Most of our moral endeavors are concerned with specific duties without much thought about the basic grounds of obligation. Granted that these duties receive their justification from some all-inclusive end such as greatest happiness, self-realization, etc., the relation of the subordinate objectives to the final end presents a problem whose solution requires the employment of the methods of science. In a very large proportion of cases it matters little which of the various final ends of moral conduct are chosen. It is the subordinate ends which are striven for that are much more important.

The medical practitioner is of course a practical moralist. The end to whose achievement his activities are directed he may express, at least for the sake of the argument, by the single word "health." Fortunately for suffering humanity, physicians have not spent most of their time in writing learned dissertations on what health consists in, or in expounding the theological implications that may be derived from that particular object of value. There is, to be sure, some opportunity for controversy over the precise way in which health should be defined. As a subordinate end of endeavor, being a *sine qua non* of desirable life, it is of sufficient importance and inclusiveness to constitute a very large part of any final moral end one is likely to set up. For a long time the application of scientific methods for the attainment of health was tabooed. The business of healing was exclusively the prerogative of the priestly caste. Diseases were attributed to magical forces or possession by supernatural agencies, and only the magical power possessed by the priests could overcome their malign influences. The theory of demoniacal possession and the treatments appropriate thereto prevailed during most of the Christian era, and its legitimate descendants are still with us. Genuine progress in the healing arts began only when the employment of scientific methods came to supplant treatment by magic or appeals to supernatural beings. The great boon to humanity that resulted from its spectacular achievements requires no comment.

The close association of any scientific discipline with theology has always proved to be an obstacle to progress. Ethics has kept up its close association longer than most fields of human knowledge. Its attempts at emancipation have elicited much the same condemnation and expressions of alarm that characterized the growing independence of the natural sciences. But, has moral science anything more to fear than medical science from its transfer of filiation or, if it has something to lose, will not its losses be more than compensated by its gains? One cannot expect anything comparable to the phenomenal achievements in the healing art, but one can legitimately expect that much light will be thrown on moral problems by the same methods that have been so successfully employed in medicine and other branches of science.

Ethics has plenty of problems belonging specifically in its own field, such as lying, fighting, sex relations, and the proper conduct of groups toward one another. In order to solve them aright, we need to know how people actually behave, why they behave as they do, and how they came to behave in these ways. We need to have much the same *kind* of understanding of moral behavior that we have of the behavior of our bodily machinery and the reasons why it often goes wrong. It is evident, I think, that the knowledge of ethics that is of most worth is the knowledge which helps us to solve the specific moral problems that present themselves. To this end, we require, as in the healing art, a scientific understanding of the human creature with which we deal.

If we assume that ethics is, as defined by Sidgwick, "The

science or study of what ought to be, so far as this depends upon the voluntary actions of individuals," we must concede that what ought to be is very commonly determined by what is. That I ought to bring a certain book to Jones depends, along with other things, on the fact that I borrowed it. Our duties in general are shaped by the circumstances in which we are placed. I shall make no attempt here to discuss the much mooted question of the relation of the "is" and the "ought". Whatever position one is likely to take in this connection, he would be very frequently compelled to employ the methods of science in order to learn what the "ought" is.

As to my own standpoint on morals, I may explain that it is entirely naturalistic. I look upon the phenomena of the moral life as explicable in the sense that this term can be applied to any phenomenon in the realm of nature. Moral problems must be solved by scientific methods, like the problems of the physiologist or the student of economics. Moral customs and standards are viewed as having had a perfectly natural genesis, like the configuration of our bodies. Whatever metaphysical or theological deductions may be legitimately drawn conformable to this standpoint I am not here concerned with. This position, I believe, expresses the attitude of the majority of scientific men. It would readily be admitted by many philosophers who would probably have no trouble in reconciling it with a variety of metaphysical and religious viewpoints. It expresses a very natural and inevitable extension of the claims of science as set forth by Tyndall in his celebrated Belfast Address, in which he stated somewhat belligerently, "We claim and shall wrest from theology the entire domain of cosmological theory." To this it is now appropriate to add, if it is not included in the term cosmological, the entire domain of social and moral theory. This change, so far as it has been effected, has been productive of most beneficial results, and holds out promises of much greater achievements. Professor John Dewey, who has striven to divest ethics of its old trappings by which its effectiveness has long been handicapped, says of ethics: "It is ineradicably empirical, not theological, nor metaphysical, nor mathematical. Since it directly concerns human nature, everything that can be known of the human mind and body in physiology, medicine, anthropology, and psychology is pertinent to moral inquiry. . . . Moral science is not a separate science, it is physical, biological and historic knowledge placed in a human context where it will illuminate and guide the activities of men."

In the field of moral conduct we sorely need the kind of enlightenment that can come only through the application of the methods of scientific research. Such enlightenment not only enables us to realize the ends we choose, but it can render valuable service in the choice of ends. It is commonly assumed that there is one all-inclusive end, or standard by which every act having moral significance can be evaluated. But as to what the true standard is, and what the terms good, bad, right, and wrong really mean and imply, one finds a remarkable amount of disagreement among moral philosophers that has persisted since the period of early Greek speculative thought and shows no perceptible sign of drawing toward a close. Some of the chief views on these topics I have briefly set forth in the next chapter for the sake of affording a general setting for the discussions which follow. The ground covered is, of course, very familiar to all who have read extensively in the literature on ethics. They will be tempted to skip my expository presentations, which they may well do, but many of them will doubtless find grounds for disagreement with some of my conclusions set forth in the latter part of the chapter.

CHAPTER III

Conflicting Moral Standards and Theories

All progress toward a system of morals capable of standing the strain of modern civilization has been toward a scientific morality; that is toward a natural morality.
—W. E. RITTER, *Bulletin of the Scripps Institution*, No. 2

LONG BEFORE MEN BEGAN to philosophize about the intrinsic nature of right and wrong they had their very definite regulations for the guidance of conduct. As a rule primitive peoples take morality very seriously, although their practices may at times prove to be shocking to our own sensibilities. Traditional mores are followed much as we commonly follow rules of etiquette without inquiring into the reasons why the rules exist. The savage is convinced that if he violates a tribal regulation something disagreeable may happen to him, and that is enough. His morality consists in obedience to authority whether it be imposed by his tribe or the supernatural beings who form an important part of the social order to which he must adjust himself.

Early notions about morals are closely associated with religious beliefs. In a number of the systems of theological ethics that have come down from ancient civilizations, acts are considered right or wrong simply because they have been so decreed by divine authority. A perfectly typical illustration of such authoritarian ethics is furnished by the code of the ancient Hebrews. According to Exodus the Ten Commandments were given to Moses by Jehovah, and supplementing these there were numerous regulations detailed in Leviticus, Deuteronomy and other books of the Old Testament by which the Children of Israel were instructed as to what they might and might not eat, how burnt offerings were to be conducted, how slaves should be purchased, sold and disciplined, the pawning of raiment, the treatment of boils, the style of cutting the beard, the breeding of cattle, and many other matters which the faithful were supposed to observe with scrupulous care.

The ethics of the Hebrews in their semibarbaric period presents a striking example of clan ethics which is most instructive to all students of the history of ethical thought and the natural history of morals. Moral commands were revealed for the special benefit of the Children of Israel. Peoples having other gods were decidedly in disfavor. The poor Hittites, Girgashites, Amorites, Canaanites, Perizzites, Hivites and Jebusites were delivered into the hands of the Israelites with the command, "Thou shalt smite them, and utterly destroy them; thou shalt make no covenant with them, nor shew mercy unto them: ... Ye shall destroy their altars ... with fire." Being worshipers of other gods, these unfortunate peoples were simply outside the pale; nothing could be too bad for them. Jehovah's chosen people, on the other hand, at least so long as they were loyal and obedient, were rewarded with victories, power and booty taken from their enemies. It behooved the faithful Hebrew to walk in the way of the Lord. That was morality.

It is quite natural that a tribe of predatory nomads like the Children of Israel should develop a code of this clannish type and ascribe to their god the qualities and conduct attributed to Jehovah. Living in the midst of tribal warfare, the

Children of Israel were prone to believe that Jehovah shared their antagonism to their enemies and looked with favor on the atrocities committed in the course of their wars. Theirs was the morality of a fighting people. Hence their god commanded one kind of conduct toward their own kind and a quite different conduct toward alien tribes.

In the Psalms, the Proverbs, and the Prophets the moral teachings of the Jews were on a distinctly higher level than in the predatory period of their history, but they remained no less authoritarian in character. In the Old Testament there is no philosophizing over the fundamental basis of morals such as we find among the ancient Greeks. Morality was conceived to grow out of a sort of fatherly relation of God to his children. God's will was the source of moral codes as parental authority may be considered as the source of morality by the child. Beyond this rather simple and naive philosophy of morals the ancient Hebrew did not attempt to go. Hence Jewish ethics was essentially legalistic in character. Questions of right and wrong were to be decided by reference to a divinely revealed command, as questions of law are decided by reference to some statute without raising any question as to why the statute exists. God being all-wise and kindly disposed toward his children, it was practically futile to speculate as to the reasons for his decrees. The law being given, man's duty was to obey and to live in a spirit of gratitude and devotion to his Creator.

This conception of man's intimate filial relationship to God was a source of profound religious satisfaction to the Jews, as it has been to many other peoples. It was the inspiration of many beautiful passages of the Old Testament, especially in the Psalms and the Prophets, which have appealed so strongly to countless readers of the Bible. There can be no doubt that it has furnished potent incentives to moral conduct and to the development of kindly feelings between man and man.

As the Jews advanced in cultural development their ideas of morality broadened; Jehovah became less harsh and vindictive, less concerned over the petty details of ceremonial observances, and less provincial in his sympathies and interests. From a tribal deity of rather uncertain temper he had evolved into the one god, the creator and ruler of the universe, solicitous above all for the righteousness of his children. This development doubtless had much to do with shaping the religious conceptions and moral teachings of the Founder of Christianity, much as the world owes to the originality of this great moral teacher. With the advent of Christianity ethics became emancipated from its narrow formalism. Emphasis was placed on purity of heart and love of fellow men of all ranks and nations, but for Jesus, quite as much as for the Prophets, the basis of morality was the divine will. Jesus did not indulge in philosophical speculations on the intrinsic nature of right and wrong. He did not employ dialectical argumentation in his popular discourses nor in his talks with his disciples. He taught "as one that had authority, and not as the scribes."

The conception of morality as obedience to the divine will has long been dominant in Christian ethics and persists in many adherents down to the present time. In the latter part of the Middle Ages and during the Renaissance the study of Greek philosophy began to stimulate speculation on the nature of good and evil. The remarkable development of philosophical thought in ancient Greece led to the promulgation of various types of ethical theory. The emphasis on reason by Greek thinkers as a means of obtaining ideal moral ends exercised an important influence on the development of ethical ideas in the Western world. Knowledge of the ethical teachings of Plato, Aristotle, and other Greek and Roman moralists tended to wrest ethics in a measure from its complete domination by authority and to give it the status of a rational system. Thomas Aquinas, who employed his great talents in the endeavor to effect a harmonious blend of Aristotelianism with Christian dogma, sought the basis of ethics not exclusively in the expressed will of God, in that there are rational sanctions for moral conduct as well as those based on revelation.

After the Renaissance, owing to the increase of knowledge and the growing independence of thought, the conception of a rationalistic system of ethics spread more widely. Among the attempts to hit upon a general criterion by which conduct can be adjudged good or bad, it was natural that appeal was often made to the pleasure or happiness arising from the act. This occurred among the Greeks, and after the revival of learning the recurrence of hedonistic doctrines in Western Europe was virtually inevitable. Thomas Hobbes, for instance, contended that man is actuated only by self-interest in all his acts. "Good and evil," he tells us, "are names that signify our appetites and aversions. No man giveth but with intention of good to himself, because gift is voluntary; and of all voluntary acts, the object to every man is his own good." Everything we do, therefore, is from selfish motives in which we seek to secure our own pleasure or to avoid pain. Being thus constituted, men are only constrained to live together more or less decently through fear of the law or the incentives of enlightened self-interest. Goodness for Hobbes really resolved itself into prudent self-seeking, and vice into following the wrong kind of pleasures.

The skeptics of the seventeenth and especially the eighteenth century were prone to adopt a hedonistic attitude in ethics. But even so stalwart a defender of the faith as the Reverend William Paley made happiness the true end of good conduct. "What promotes the public happiness, or happiness upon the whole," says Paley, "is agreeable to the fitness of things, to nature, to reason, and to truth, and such is the divine character that what promotes the general happiness is required by the will of God; and what has all the above properties must needs be right." By pursuing the design argument as he successfully employed it in his celebrated *Natural Theology,* Paley contended that God evidently designed man to be happy, and hence, if we follow the utilitarian standard, we are naturally led to obey God's will. In Paley's conception we have at once a naturalistic and an authoritarian ethics. Through revelation we are given further aid to the discovery of right conduct beyond what we might learn through our unaided reason and experience.

Paley's attempt to reconcile natural and theological ethics was not followed by the majority of Christian moralists. Happiness was conceded to be a very nice thing to have and a quite appropriate reward of merit, but few of them went so far as to enthrone it as the supreme end of human conduct. Shaftesbury, Hutcheson, Hume and Adam Smith treated happiness as the end of moral endeavor, although not always with entire consistency, but it was Jeremy Bentham, "the father of English utilitarianism," who stands forth as a most vigorous and enthusiastic champion of the greatest happiness of the greatest number as the one all-important principle which can bring order out of chaos in ethics and politics. He was the first to attempt to apply quantitative methods to ethical and political problems. He believed that we are really all utilitarians whether we think so or not, for he maintained that mankind "is under the governance of two sovereign masters, pain and pleasure." They not only determine what is right and what is wrong, but "they govern us in all we do, in all we say, in all we think." They are the impelling forces which decide every act of the will. We follow pleasure and avoid pain simply because we must.

To ascertain whether an act is right or wrong one has to balance its pleasurable and painful effects on all parties concerned, both present and future. If pleasures outweigh pains in the hedonic calculus the act is right; otherwise it is wrong. In order that they may be balanced correctly pleasures and pains must be considered from the standpoint of their intensity, their duration, and the number of individuals affected. Pleasures and pains are, of course, susceptible of only very rough measurement, but the standard affords at least a theoretically possible way of deciding moral problems by quantitative methods.

One of the arguments against utilitarianism, which is found in almost every modern textbook on ethics, is directed against the assumption expressed by Mill that, "Happiness is desirable and the only thing desirable as an end; all other things being only desirable as means to this end." This also is the doctrine of Bentham, but is it good psychology? Most psychologists tell us "No." We strive to attain objectives quite regardless of their pleasurable or painful effects. A mother bear alarmed by her cub's cry of distress and rushing to its defense is surely actuated by no considerations of pleasure or pain. She acts impulsively on the basis of her maternal instinct. Under similar circumstances a human mother might act in the same way for the same fundamental reason. William James, in commenting on the doctrine we are discussing, remarks, "Important as the influence of pleasures and pains upon our movements are, they are far from being our only stimuli. With the manifestations of instinct and emotional expression, for example, they have absolutely nothing to do. Who smiles for the pleasure of smiling, or frowns for the pleasure of the frown? Who blushes to escape from the discomfort of not blushing? Or who in anger, grief, or fear is actuated for the movements which he makes by the pleasures which they yield? In all these cases the movements are discharged fatally by the *vis a tergo* which the stimulus exerts upon a nervous system framed to respond in just that way."

The doctrine that in all our acts we are impelled by the desire to gain pleasure or avoid pain afforded an attractively simple conception of human motivation that appealed strongly to the rationalists and skeptics, and it is quite natural that d'Holbach, Helvetius, Mandeville, Bentham and the Mills made it the basis of their explanations of human behavior. It had to be conceded that human beings are so constituted that they willingly perform kindly and generous acts, but it was claimed that such acts are performed because of the pleasure they afford the doer or in anticipation of future pleasures in return. Those who looked upon man as essentially egoistic had to appeal to some external force to induce him to promote the welfare of his fellows. For this task Hobbes invoked the coercive power of the state. Bentham similarly regarded it as the chief business of government, but in addition to legislation he relied on the force of public opinion to which even the most selfish must give some heed. Between fear of the law and regard for the approbation or disapprobation of his fellows, man may get along passably well in a properly regulated state. But human nature being as it is, legislators require all the assistance they can obtain from authorities on the arts of government. Hence considerations of practical politics occupy a prominent place in the writings of Hobbes, Bentham, the Mills, and other utilitarians.

The principle of utility was especially attractive to Bentham because it seemed to afford a scientific basis for legislation. The gross injustices and corruption growing out of the administration of English law fully deserved the scathing indictments they received in Bentham's writings as they did later in the novels of Charles Dickens. The whole system of law, it was claimed, should be revised according to the principle of utility. Unquestionably Bentham's influence contributed to make law more rational and humane, not only in England but in other countries.

Although utilitarianism has incurred many reproaches, including the epithet "pig philosophy" bestowed by Thomas Carlyle, it was developed in a spirit of humanity and social reform. "I am a selfish man," wrote Bentham, "as selfish as any man can be. But in me, somehow or other, so it happens, selfishness has taken the shape of benevolence." Nowadays most psychologists would, I think, disagree with Bentham's evaluation of his own motives. Champions of equal rights, like Bentham and J. S. Mill, were strongly attracted to the utilitarian principle on account of its democratic implications. "As between his own happiness and that of others," says Mill, "utilitarianism requires him to be as strictly impartial as a disinterested and benevolent spectator. In the golden rule of Jesus of Nazareth, we read the complete spirit of the ethics of utility."

In the distribution of the greatest happiness to the greatest number Bentham's rule is, "Everybody to count for one and nobody for more than one." It would follow that the happiness of a king should be given no more weight in the hedonistic calculus than that of the meanest beggar or the vilest criminal. From a purely quantitative standpoint one would, in consistency, have to consider the lower animals as well as human beings. If ten rats could derive more enjoyment out of life than one man, and if the extinction of the human race would occasion more than a tenfold increase in the number of rats so as to produce a greater sum total of positive pleasure, and this condition were to persist indefinitely, then it would seem to be the duty of the human race to extinguish itself and allow the rats to overrun the earth.

This illustration will serve to bring out a very common source of antagonism to utilitarian ethics. It is the feeling that pleasure is all very well in its way, but it is hardly worthy of being held up as the highest goal of human conduct. People associate pleasure with the satisfactions of eating, drinking, and other forms of sensuous enjoyment. Mere pleasure seekers are not regarded as the noblest types of humanity. The feeling of the unworthiness of the pursuit of pleasure is so strong in some people of an ascetic turn of mind that they look upon nearly all kinds of enjoyment as almost sinful. The Puritans of the time of Charles II were strongly opposed to dancing and pleasurable games, and regarded it "a sin to hang garlands on a Maypole, to drink a friend's health, to fly a hawk, to hunt a stag, to play at chess, to wear love-locks, to put starch in a ruff, to touch the virginals, to read the *Faerie Queen*"; and Macaulay elsewhere remarks that "the Puritans hated bear-baiting, not because it gave pain to the bear, but because it gave pleasure to the spectators." The Puritan spirit is naturally hostile to an ethics based on the greatest happiness principle, especially if happiness is identified with pleasure and all pleasures are rated as of equal worth. J. S. Mill, who was something of a Puritan in temperament, held that pleasures were of different degrees of worth, but Bentham, with his usual outspokenness, stuck rigidly to his guns and asserted, "Pushpin is as good as poetry provided the pleasure be as great."

This type of utilitarianism tended to repel many people of fine moral sentiments. The greatest happiness principle is more acceptable if happiness and pleasure are not used as equivalent terms. Aristotle distinguished between them. It is often said that happiness denotes a state of more permanent felicity than pleasure, or that it implies a higher kind of satisfaction (Muirhead). A good deal of the rather tedious controversy over happiness and pleasure is a mere war of words because different writers distinguish between these terms in various ways that suit their own purposes. Both refer to feelings, and, at least for normal individuals, they are feelings that people like to have. Almost all moralists, whatever views they may hold on the nature of right and wrong, admit that they are goods that may be legitimately sought, at least within reasonable limits. Most psychologists now hold that they are not the only ends sought. And if pleasure and happiness are not the exclusive objects of our striving, they cannot be the sole measures of moral conduct.

THE INTUITIONISTS

The adherents of the intuitionist school of morals hold that we know what is right and wrong on the authority of our moral sense. By some members of this school it is maintained that our moral sense not only points the way to duty, but, as expressed by Lecky, "Our knowledge of the Supreme Excellence, our best evidence even of the existence of the Creator, is derived, not from the material universe, but from our own moral nature. It is not of reason but of faith. In other words it springs from that instinctive or moral nature which is as truly a part of our being as our reason, which teaches us what reason could never teach, the supreme and transcendent excellence of the moral good."

Among British authors intuitional ethics was ardently championed by the so-called Scotch school, with whom philosophy was very much the handmaid of theology, and also by Bishop Butler, Price, Whewell, and a multitude of later writers. Of the Scotch school neither Reid, Dugald Stewart, nor Thomas Brown went so far as to claim that the moral sense, or conscience, is always an infallible guide to goodness. Although Reid claimed, "in order to know what is right and wrong in human conduct, we need only listen to the dictates of conscience when the mind is calm and unruffled," he realized that at times the inner light is very dim and flickering. And Brown stated that if a man were drunk his moral sense might become quite untrustworthy. We are so constituted, it was claimed, that we approve of certain acts and disapprove of others, but since we are all imperfect vessels and differ in temperament, character and wisdom, these differences color our opinions somewhat as to right and wrong, but under most conditions the path of duty was held to be clear.

Intuitionism, as usually expounded, involves an appeal, indirectly if not directly, to supernatural authority. We are held to be endowed by our Creator with a faculty which enables us, with the aid of a little knowledge and reflection, it may be, to perceive what is right and what is wrong. Such a view is akin to the old-fashioned notion of instinct as a power supernaturally implanted in animals which tells them, independently of experience, how to conduct their lives. If a spider knows *a priori* how to spin its web, one might conclude that a man might know *a priori* how to choose the good and avoid evil. And since instinct, admittedly an innate faculty, is not always infallible, an occasional error of the moral sense should not be considered as a fatal objection to its intuitive nature.

It cannot be maintained, without begging the question, that our acts are right if we think they are right, and no one can deny that conscience approves of acts whose effects are thoroughly bad. In any workable system of morals the effects of conduct have to be given weight in evaluating it as right or wrong. Utilitarianism has come in for much criticism on account of the difficulty of balancing all the pleasures that result from any act. But any theory that evaluates conduct, even partially, on the basis of its consequences encounters a similar difficulty. Every act starts a series of causes and effects that continues without end. It is quite possible, therefore, that the remote effects of our conduct might outweigh any proximate ones that could reasonably be estimated. Hence we can never be *entirely* sure that any of our acts are right. To affirm that our moral sense gives us reliable knowledge of the total effects of our actions is indeed to ascribe to it supernatural powers.

In relation to murder, lying, stealing, and a few other acts to which popular thought commonly, but erroneously, restricts the sphere of moral significance, our conscientious scruples work very well in making conduct subservient to social welfare. But in many of the problems that confront us in our everyday lives we have no reliable inner guide as to what is the right thing to do. Our conscience may bid us do the best we can, but that gives us no surety that what we do will not be bad.

THE CATEGORICAL IMPERATIVE

In this brief survey of theories on the nature of right and wrong I should not omit all consideration of Kant's doctrine of the categorical imperative, but I approach the subject with some misgivings, for I cannot in a short space do justice to the ethical teachings of this great philosopher nor to their articulation with the rest of his metaphysical system. I shall confine my few remarks, therefore, mainly to one aspect of the Kantian ethics.

According to Kant, we are in possession of a faculty, however we may have come by it, that bids us unequivocally to obey its commands. The laws of the realm may forbid our selling intoxicating liquors or playing cards on a train. Such laws are said to be contingent, since they depend upon the attitudes and opinions of the ruling powers of the state. If we violate them we may incur a penalty. But the law within us which commands us to follow the path of duty is, according to Kant, independent of the accidents of our environment. Duty, "stern daughter of the voice of God," commands us unconditionally.

But what does she command us to do? Nothing specifically. Kant is much less specific than the author or authors of Leviticus. He gives us a formula of the most general character. It is, "Act according to that maxim only which you can wish at the same time to become a universal law." If you are tempted to steal a purse, to use an illustration of Kant, you should reflect what would happen if everyone were to steal purses. Your own purse would be unsafe. Hence your conduct, if made a general rule, would result in inconsistencies. It is the inconsistencies, or inner contradictions, of such acts that make them wrong. Bad acts are like fallacies in logic. We must follow rules of reason if we attain truth. Similarly we must follow the commands of the categorical imperative to obey a principle of reason if we attain goodness.

It should be pointed out that to act as one would like everyone else to act might sometimes lead to curious results. Some individuals would have us all nudists, others all Adventists, Mormons, Holy Rollers, or members of the Communist party. All these people may be very well-meaning in their endeavors to universalize conduct, but since they would do it in different ways they cannot all be right. There would still be inconsistencies resulting from conflicting aims. Obviously the kind of conduct one would like to see universally followed would depend upon his outlook, temperament and various other influences besides. The element of contingency enters into all our moral problems. To brush it aside would be a disservice to morality.

As a practical working system Kant's formal ethics suffers from many imperfections which have been pointed out by Hegel, Green, Bradley, Caird, Seth, Sidgwick, Rashdall, Dewey, and many other critics. Perhaps the chief weakness of the Kantian ethics lies in its faulty psychology. When we speak of something within us that issues unconditional commands, we are using highly figurative language. Let anyone attend to his mental states when he is impelled to do something from a sense of duty. There is first of all a feeling of oughtness, which is evidently emotional in character, accompanied by an impulse to perform an act that is judged to be right. Just what are the components of this feeling of oughtness is a psychological problem which presents many difficulties of introspective analysis. The make-up of this feeling would doubtless vary greatly from case to case. Sympathy, pride, shame, self-respect, and other components may enter into it in varying proportions. If we did not have these feelings no one would ever have thought about duty or obligation, nor endeavored to found duty on an abstract principle of reason. But to use these familiar emotional experiences, as Kant did, as a basis for *a priori* general principles of morals and for the deduction of fundamental metaphysical and theological doctrines, is to build upon a very weak and unsafe psychological foundation.

Kant endeavored to found ethics on the solid rock of *a priori* truth. Its fundamental principles, he thought, cannot be shaken by anything that may happen in the outside world. Through the vicissitudes of life duty points out the way to righteousness and bids us follow duty for duty's sake. "Duty," Kant exclaims, "wondrous thought, that workest neither by fond insinuation, flattery, nor by any threat, but merely holding up thy naked law in the soul and so extorting for thyself always reverence, if not always obedience; before whom appetites are dumb, however secretly they rebel; whence thy original?" But is the noble sentiment expressed in this celebrated passage based on good psychology? I more than doubt it.

Instead of basing ethics on the observation of the facts of human conduct, and endeavoring to reduce these to some sort of a rational system, Kant abandons the inductive for the *a priori* method and endeavors to *deduce* his conclusions as to what is right or wrong without deigning to consider anything but the *a priori* principle from which conduct should spring. "When we are dealing with nature," says Kant, "experience must be our rule, as it is the source of all true knowledge; but when we are dealing with morality, experience is, sad to say, the mother of illusion, and the thought is utterly to be reprobated that we should gather the laws for what we ought to do from that which is actually done, or limit the former to the latter." "Kant wished," Caird says, "to purify the moral consciousness of all empirical elements." "All moral conceptions," Kant declares, "have their seat and origin completely *a priori* in the reason, and it is just this purity of their origin that makes them worthy to serve as our supreme practical principle."

It is because of the *a priori* derivation of his principles that Kant has been so generally criticized for giving us nothing but a blank formula that breaks down when one attempts to apply it in practice. It is pleasures, pains, loves, hopes, fears, ambitions and desires that afford the very meat and bone of any ethics that is to be of great value to humanity, as was forcibly brought out by Jacobi in his strictures on the Kantian position. Kant attempted to get rid of them as contingent matter that can only bring confusion in a moral philosophy based on pure reason. In mathematics it may be feasible to proceed by the *a priori* method alone. There one deals with deductions from fundamental postulates. But, of all subjects, a science concerned with the behavior of men, women and children under all the varied conditions of their lives is compelled to make constant appeals to experience to discover the right and the wrong things to do.

THE STANDARD OF SELF-REALIZATION

The doctrine that the true standard of good conduct is some form of self-realization has been widely adopted, especially by idealist philosophers who have been strongly influenced by Hegel. One of the most elaborate expositions of this standpoint is made by T. H. Green in his *Prolegomena to Ethics* which has exerted a marked influence over the development of English ethical thought. The doctrine has enlisted the support of many able adherents among whom may be mentioned Bradley, Seth, Muirhead, MacKenzie, Sorley, E. Caird, Wallace, McTaggart, and Royce. One encounters much variation in the way in which self-realization is conceived and applied and also much vagueness in the idea. It is repeatedly pointed out that self-realization does not imply an egoistic standpoint because the self, or as some prefer to say, the true self, can only be realized through its harmonious and helpful cooperation with other selves. Mr. Bradley, for instance, states in his *Ethical Studies,* "If my self which I aim at is the realization in me of a moral world which is a system of selves, an organism in which I am a member, and in whose life I live—then I cannot aim at my own well-being without aiming at that of the others. The others are not means to me, but are involved in my essence."

Here, as elsewhere in Bradley's able volume, there is involved the idea of a sort of metaphysical identity of one's self with the selves of others. This is a favorite escape from the egoistic implications of the doctrine. It amounts to saying that you and I are not altogether different persons after all. In some deep, metaphysical sense we are all one, even if we are deadly enemies; and all of us are one with the Absolute. A similar idea is expressed by Sorley in speaking of "a unity of self-consciousness which transcends the differences by which concrete individuals are distinguished from one another."

In the interpretation given it by most Neo-Hegelians, self-realization means much more than it says. As Kant has built extensively on the foundation of the categorical imperative, writers of the perfectionist school deduce far-reaching conclusions from the concept of self-realization, but a consideration of the metaphysical implications of the doctrine is foreign to our present task. There is nothing particularly meritorious about self-realization conceived simply as a development of one's own capacities. If I should become a murderous gangster, I should realize possibilities of development which might be brought out more readily through membership in an organized gang who, to a greater degree than most other individuals, would share what Mr. Bradley would call "the same essence." Dean Rashdall has remarked, "Morality is self-realization beyond a doubt, but then, so is immorality."

Those who set up the standard of self-realization naturally interpret it in accordance with common-sense morality. For this purpose the vagueness of the idea admirably adapts it. One may conceive it as full and effective living, or what Spencer calls "completeness of life." He may hold this can only be attained by working in harmony with the lives of others, and he may avoid becoming involved with the metaphysical and transcendental notions with which the idea has been so frequently associated. But however much of community of interest there may be among people in organized society, circumstances may arise in which the self-realization of an individual interferes with that of his neighbors. One may attempt to escape from admitting the reality of such dilemmas by saying that any kind of antisocial conduct would not be the fulfillment of the "true self." The adherents of this viewpoint have a number of selves at their disposal, such as the private self, the universal self, the self of ideal perfection, and are thus able to construe as self-realization almost any conduct that meets with their moral approval. But into the subtleties of the discussion of such topics I must forbear to enter.

THE DARWINIAN STANDARD

The theory of organic evolution is consistent with a variety of doctrines concerning the good and the nature of moral obligation. Much of the ethics that is called evolutionary is basically utilitarian. This is conspicuously true of the ethics of Herbert Spencer. But one's views on certain matters of ethical theory would inevitably be affected by the particular hypothesis he adopts as to how evolution is caused, provided, of course, he is consistent in following the implications of his standpoint.

Since, according to the theory of natural selection, all the native endowments of man owe their development to their conduciveness to survival, a Darwinian would be disposed to regard as good, acts which favor the life and welfare of the individual or the species, and to regard as bad, acts which have the reverse effect. This is, as one might expect, essentially the standard adopted by Darwin. He never developed this phase of his doctrine fully, but in the course of a brief discussion of the greatest happiness principle he makes the following significant statement: "The term general good may be defined as the rearing of the greatest possible number of individuals in full vigour and health, with all their faculties perfect, under the conditions to which they are subjected. As the social instincts, both of man and the lower animals, have no doubt been developed by nearly the same steps, it would be advisable, if found practicable, to use the same definition in both cases, and to take as the standard the general good or welfare of the community rather than the general happiness."

Probably Darwin would have included happiness as an important constituent of welfare. Evolutionists commonly adopt a dual standard by which conduct is evaluated in terms of feelings aroused and also in terms of the biological effects produced. Theoretically a behaviorist might disregard consciousness in ethics as completely as he attempts to do in psychology, but feeling simply cannot be ignored in any ethical system worthy of serious consideration. In the early chapters of his *Data of Ethics,* Spencer is at some pains to show that there is no real antagonism between the biological and the psychological criteria of conduct. This is because "It is demonstrable that there exists a primordial connection between pleasure-giving acts and continuance or increase of life, and by implication between pain-giving acts and decrease or loss of life," and "if we contemplate developed creatures as now existing, we see that each individual and species is from day to day kept alive by pursuit of the agreeable and avoidance of the disagreeable." This association between the pleasurable and the beneficial and between the painful and the injurious is no pre-established harmony, but one which, according to Spencer, owes its origin to the fact that "there must ever have been, other things equal, the most numerous and long-continued survivals among races in which these adjustments of feelings to actions were the best, tending ever to bring about perfect adjustment."

Having thus been established through natural selection these adjustments must, from the nature of the case, be more or less loose. Indeed, Spencer concedes, as he obviously must, that "since the conditions of existence for each species have been occasionally changing, there have been occasionally arising partial mis-adjustments of the feelings to the requirements, necessitating re-adjustments," and he goes on to state that "this general cause of derangement operating on all sentient beings has been operating on human beings in a manner especially decided, persistent and involved."

The critics of Spencer have, of course, made much out of the possible antagonism of the biological and the psychological standards of conduct. Sorley questioned whether the evolutionary, or rather the Spencerian, conclusion that human evolution involves an increase of happiness is demonstrably true. If a simpler and more primitive life should yield more happiness than a life that is more highly evolved it would follow that, as Sorley stated, "we must make our choice between evolutionism and hedonism."

Throughout his writings Spencer was under the spell of a concept of evolution as a process going majestically onward from an indefinite, incoherent homogeneity to a definite, coherent heterogeneity as a result of general laws formulated in his *First Principles*. Given these laws, evolution must proceed all the way from primitive nebulae to the social and moral development of man. This deductive derivation of the law of evolution was quite foreign to the thinking of Darwin. The direction of evolution, according to Darwin, is at the beck and call of opportunity. It may be upward, downward, or sidewise, as conditions determine the most advantageous path to follow. In many environments an increase in complexity would be a drawback. This kind of development an evolutionist would be under no obligation to promote.

It cannot be maintained, therefore, that following the biological or the psychological standard would always and everywhere lead to the same conduct. For practical purposes the differences might be negligible, but whether they were small or great, one would have to choose between the two standards. Spencer leaves no doubt as to what choice he would make. "Since . . . the justification for whatever increases life is the reception from life of more happiness than misery; it follows that conduciveness to happiness is the ultimate test of perfection in a man's nature." With all his devotion to the doctrine of evolution Spencer was first and foremost a utilitarian.

BY WHAT STANDARD SHALL WE CHOOSE BETWEEN STANDARDS?

People differ a great deal over matters of right and wrong, and they often justify their opinions by an appeal to this or that standard. Each standard, once adopted, supplies a principle by which their differences may, at least theoretically, be decided. But where differences over standards are involved, each disputant would naturally oppose the standard of the other on the basis of the correctness of his own. In such controversies the opportunities for begging the question are obviously excellent. Is there any way out of the vicious circle?

In one sense, since ethics is concerned with action, the choice of a standard is a purely voluntary matter. Being a free moral agent, I may order my life in accordance with the dictates of egoistic hedonism, the greatest happiness principle, or any other standard that suits my fancy. My decision may finally rest upon a matter of taste, like my choice between beefsteak and pork chops. In what sense then can I be said to be wrong about morals any more than about food? Like aesthetic judgments, moral judgments are based on conceptions of value. To me Mary Jones may be a very beautiful girl, but my friend Smith, who thinks she is homely, may try to convince me that I am wrong by pointing out that Mary has freckles and a turned-up nose that I may not have noticed; but if I find freckles pleasing and like turned-up noses, Smith's argument loses all its force. My differences with

Smith may rest finally on a purely emotional basis. No amount of logical argument can force us to agree simply because we are different human beings.

Let us imagine a spider trying to convince a bee that she ought to spend her time spinning web instead of collecting honey. According to the respective standards of these creatures a good spider is one that spins her web well, and a good bee is one that collects honey well. But neither could convince the other of the error of its ways because the premises of each are established by instinct. Obviously the instincts of Smith and myself differ far less than those of a spider and a bee, but they differ a little, and to the extent that these differences influence judgments of value and hence our moral aims, our controversies cannot be settled by argument. Judgments of value in morals, being strongly influenced by emotions, agree in the main largely because people are emotionally much alike. Considerations that guide us in our everyday conduct influence our general theory by which our acts are evaluated. Our standards are shaped by what appeals to us; and what appeals to us must meet our emotional as well as our intellectual requirements.

An adherent of Darwinian ethics might contend, however: "I cannot prevent you from setting up any standard you choose and acting accordingly, but my standard, to speak figuratively, has the approval of Nature. Whatever cause people may assign as to why stealing is wrong, whether the reason be the will of their gods, experiences of unhappiness caused by the act, or whatever else, the real reason for their condemnation of stealing is that it leads to a loss of social integration and endangers survival. Morality is life-preserving conduct. Too great a departure from the code of Nature spells extinction. Hence we must obey Nature and promote her end of enhancing life or it will be the worse for us. Nature has brought morality into the world by the same evolutionary process by which she has developed countless other adaptations in animals and plants. From the Darwinian standpoint morality becomes affiliated with life in general of which it is merely the crown. It is true life."

And to the hedonists and utilitarians he might say: "The pursuit of happiness for one's self or for others would prove disastrous were it not for the fact that through the operation of natural selection human beings have become so constituted that what brings them happiness contributes, by and large, to their biological welfare. Animals were made to behave in ways that help them to live, and their hedonistic propensities were developed as useful adjuncts to this end. Pleasure or happiness is just Nature's bait to lure sentient creatures to follow the Darwinian standard when they think they are simply seeking their own satisfactions. They even make great sacrifices to promote the welfare of their kind and enjoy doing it."

While the Darwinian would explain the development of morality as due to its conduciveness to survival, by no means all acts that bring moral approval are performed because of their survival value. Being an intelligent creature and doing all sorts of things as a consequence of his erroneous notions and foolish fancies, man has inevitably given moral approval to many kinds of conduct which are positively harmful to himself and his group. These imperfections are comparable to the nonadaptiveness and even the maladaptiveness which, to a limited extent, characterizes all the processes of life. It is only in a very broad and general sense, therefore, that the moral practices of people owe their origin to their conduciveness to survival. One should not employ the theory of natural selection to explain why orthodox Jews think it a sin to eat pork any more than to account for the distribution of freckles on a boy's face.

Darwinism is essentially a theory of how living things

came to be as they are: i.e., it is a way of interpreting history. But the fact that I am a product of a certain method of development does not *logically* compel me to adopt any one standard of conduct rather than another. Darwinism may explain why I am moral and why the standard I adopt is largely Darwinian as most standards really are. It gives me a concept of an end of action which is in harmony with the goal toward which Nature's processes have been trending. But if I do not like the goal, no logic can force me to approve it. All the long controversies over moral standards are like arguments over matters of taste, and they involve question-begging throughout.

The futility of the quest for the one true standard of morals is finally coming to be recognized by a number of writers on ethics. Prominent among these is E. Westermarck, who in his recent volume on *Ethical Relativity* contended that "moral judgments are ultimately based on emotions, the moral concepts being generalizations of emotional tendencies," and that "the emotional origin of moral judgments consequently leads to a denial of the objective validity ascribed to them both by common sense and the normative theories of ethics." As interpreted by Westermarck, ethics deals with the kinds of conduct upon which people pass judgments of moral approval or disapproval. The student of ethics may describe these kinds of conduct among different peoples, as Westermarck has done in so much detail, noting their similarities and their divergences, and he may be able to discover many of the reasons for the practices that are followed. In other words, he should approach the subject, as Darwin attempted to do, from the standpoint of the naturalist. To study human conduct with a view of explaining why people act as they do is a perfectly legitimate, scientific procedure, but to determine why they *should* act in a certain way is to be concerned with one's own standards of evaluation, and these are basically emotional. For Westermarck, ethics is a branch of psychology viewed as a science of actual behavior and its conscious accompaniments.

One might urge that while we may look upon other people's conduct as so much objective material, when we decide what our own acts shall be we must employ some standard of evaluation. Here our problem is not to explain what we do, but to *determine* what we do, and if our moral life is to have any unity and consistency of aim we must order it in accordance with some principle. We may get along passably well perhaps by following what our associates approve, but this course cannot be considered as a very worthy ideal. We can only do what seems to us best as we interpret the term best. And how we interpret this term will depend upon our own nature and the environmental influences that have molded our character and outlook on life. Let us say, then, that to be morally consistent I must choose a standard, though my choice may depend finally on a matter of taste. My choice might bring me into conflict with my fellows, but an impartial observer would only commend my course. There are bound to be differences over morals and some of them cannot be resolved until differences over standards are eliminated. But the choice of a standard, although determined in part by emotion, is to a considerable degree amenable to the influence of reason and enlightenment. As defined by most liberal-minded writers on ethics at the present time, the ideal end of moral endeavor, whether the general happiness, self-realization, fullness and perfection of life, human welfare, or "universal harmony of feeling and vital activity," would, if realized, lead to much the same result.

We are getting beyond the notion that the end of moral striving is mere blind obedience to a command, or to enhance the glory of God, and few would have the hardihood to maintain that it consists in securing one's personal pleasure regardless of how others are affected. More and more the ground for moral conduct is sought in the relationships of man to man. Morality is the outgrowth of social life, and the urge to goodness rests upon the inherently good impulses of human nature. We may be assured, therefore, that its basis is stable, however greatly it may be affected by man's physical and social environment. As will be shown more in detail in the following chapters, the foundations of morality were deeply laid in the long course of man's evolution from lower forms of life. The goals of good conduct that people set up are determined by their emotions and impulses in the light of the knowledge and wisdom they have acquired. The kindly will is a product of the evolution of social groups. The wisdom for its guidance comes of necessity from experience. The moral standards we follow are the resultants of both these factors, and they reflect the development of our insight and understanding. The utilitarian outlook, the perfectionist outlook, and the Darwinian outlook have all made their contributions to ethics, both theoretical and practical. If we act better as we grow in knowledge and wisdom, the most illuminating viewpoint would naturally be of the greatest service to mankind.

But a viewpoint involves much more than a mere standard of evaluation. It influences our conduct through giving us a different conception of the nature of man and his relations to the world. In this respect especially lies the great import of the biological outlook. If we do not accept the Socratic doctrine that wisdom is the essence of virtue, we cannot deny that, according to any standard of morals that has any claims to rationality, it is a powerful aid to the good life. If we concede that the Darwinian standard of morals, like other standards, cannot be justified without begging the question, the great importance of the Darwinian theory in relation to morals would not be seriously impaired. If the theory is illuminating, if it increases our insight into the springs of human conduct and helps us to give a rational interpretation of man's social relationships and the development of his institutions, it cannot fail to be of great service to practical morality.

The obvious aim of the practical moralist is to make people behave better than they do. The task is beset with formidable difficulties but, within limits, is by no means hopeless. Thus far its accomplishment may have been disappointingly slow, but progress in overcoming our physical ills was exceedingly slow until the advent of scientific medicine when it advanced with an unprecedented pace. One is tempted to cherish, at least, the hope for a similar, if much less spectacular, result from a scientific knowledge of man's social and moral life.

RETROSPECTION AND FINAL COMMENTS

In concluding this discussion on the whys and wherefores of right and wrong, it may be useful to give a brief tabular summary of viewpoints. If a friend meets with an accident and I play the part of a good Samaritan and relieve his distress, nearly everyone would call my action right, but among the reasons why it is right one might find the following statements:

It is right because it gives me pleasure to perform it or will result in some benefit to me in return (Aristippus, Hobbes, Mandeville, Helvetius).

It is right because it increases the sum of human happiness (Bentham, Priestly, Godwin, the Mills, Spencer, Leslie Stephen, Sidgwick, and utilitarians generally).

It is right because it is in accordance with the will of God, or at least in harmony with the divine will (most ancient Hebrew and many Christian and other moralists).

It is right for both of the preceding reasons (Paley).

It is right because it was done in obedience to the categorical imperative in accordance with the requirements of reason (Kant).

It is right because it was the most reasonable and hence the most godlike thing to do (Plato, Aristotle).

It is right because it benefits the man and is in accordance with my benevolent instincts (Shaftesbury).

It is right because of objective moral laws revealed by intuition (Price, Reid, Brown, Stewart, and other intuitionists).

It is right because it promotes human welfare, not necessarily pleasure, or even happiness (Paulsen, Rashdall).

It is right because it was an act of self-realization in whatever sense of the term self one chooses to employ, from John Smith to the Absolute (Hegel, many Neo-Hegelians, and idealist metaphysicans of various persuasions).

It is right because it evokes an emotion of moral approval (Westermarck).

It is right because it makes for the fullness and perfection of life (Darwin).

It is right just because it is right (a great many plain people and some philosophers, although in somewhat different phraseology).

Most of the viewpoints mentioned in this far from exhaustive list rest upon certain assumptions concerning human nature and the relation of man to God. Authoritarian ethics as exemplified in the Bible and other assumed revelations of the divine will, the Platonic and Aristotelian conceptions of the rational nature of the good, the theory of immutable principles of right and wrong, the doctrine of conscience as a divinely implanted voice, the categorical imperative of Kant, the principle of self-realization as expounded by most Hegelians, and even utilitarian ethics as set forth by Paley,

Priestly and Austin, all, in one way or another, involve an appeal to God. The attempts to break away from the pervasive influence of theological teachings and to found ethics on a purely naturalistic basis have usually had recourse to some form of hedonism, individual or social. The cruder forms of egoistic hedonism have few defenders among present-day moralists. Utilitarianism still survives the demonstration of the faulty psychological basis with which it was supplied by Bentham and J. S. Mill. There is a growing tendency to seek the grounds for morality in some form of human welfare and to look upon moral obligation as growing out of social relationships, as is illustrated by the Darwinian and various other standpoints. But there are still differences over standards and they may persist indefinitely, although moralists tend to have more nearly the same ideals of right conduct as their outlook on life is broadened and as they arrive at a truer understanding of their world.

A number of evolutionary naturalists have maintained that conduciveness to survival is the true end of moral conduct. Mere survival, however, under very painful conditions would hardly be a desirable objective. I would prefer to say that conduciveness to survival affords a plausible reason why life-preservative conduct, and specifically conduct leading to group survival, meets with moral approval. However, acts often receive moral sanction for a variety of reasons, some of which, as I have pointed out, have no discernible relation to utility. This fact is an inevitable consequence of the possession of intelligence, especially when it operates with imperfect knowledge. Moral standards, like our standards of weights and measures, are what we make them. There may be good natural history reasons why they are made as they are, but the attempt to discover the one true and only standard for conduct, as if it were imbedded somehow in the nature of things, is a vain quest. So far as I can see, it is quite respectable to have a number of moral standards instead of being wedded indissolubly to one. The claim that moral ends all boil down to one in the last analysis cannot, I believe, be sustained. Certainly moral conduct is directed to the attainment of numerous objectives. We may derive satisfaction in accomplishing our ends, but it is the aim and not the satisfaction that for the most part directs our efforts. Ends of moral conduct comprise both feelings, such as happiness, satisfaction, or even pleasure, and also objective achievements, such as building a bridge or increasing the food supply. It may be claimed that the latter ends are morally justified only in so far as they produce desirable feelings, but this is not necessarily the reason why, as a matter of fact, these achievements are morally approved. We may concede that bridges and food would have no value if they did not result in human satisfaction. Therefore, it may be claimed that it is the resulting satisfaction that should be our aim in striving for any objective. Now when I say I *should* do a certain thing, the implication is that the act meets with my moral approval, according to the standard which I adopt. And if it is asked why I should adopt this particular standard and if I reply that it is because the effect of so doing would result in the promotion of the general happiness or satisfaction, I am simply begging the question.

J. S. Mill, in discussing the nature of proof of which the principle of greatest happiness is susceptible, came to the conclusion that since pleasure and pain afford the motivation of all our acts, we must perforce adopt the utilitarian standard. It is now pretty well recognized that Mill's argument was psychologically unsound. One may adduce biological, psychological, social or economic reasons why certain standards of morals are adopted. He may show that, in the light of widely accepted criteria, some standards are better than others. But his attempts at logical justification, as distinguished from causal explanation, rest on human judgments of value, and these vary as a result of constitutional and cultural differences. For Kant the moral law is invariable because it is grounded in the transcendental ego which is the same for all. For the intuitionists the standard of morals has a common ground in the constitution of the universe and the human soul, and for the adherents of an authoritarian ethics there is a common standard based on the will of God. For the evolutionary naturalist, however, whatever agreement there may be in moral standards is simply a result of the fact that people are mentally and physically quite similar, and have had to meet more or less similar situations during their cultural development.

Morality is coming more and more to be measured in terms of human welfare. Many ethicists look upon the promotion of welfare as superior to any other moral aim that has been set up. The connotation of the term "welfare" is more or less indefinite, which is a positive advantage. It leaves room for a variety of interpretations, and at the same time it confines them within reasonable limits. It is distinctly humanistic. It has no necessary metaphysical or theological implications beyond those which might be found for any other term. It is quite consistent with the treatment of the whole field of morals from a naturalistic standpoint. It emphasizes the social values of morality without neglecting the interests of the individual. Both the utilitarian and the Darwinian standards may be included under the broader category of the general weal. The use of this standard would tend to emancipate ethics from the shackles of formalism and its domination by authority, and to set less store by adherence to rules and more upon the basic human virtue of kindness. It would emphasize the importance of learning more about the conditions upon which human welfare depends and of paying more heed to these conditions among other nations and peoples. Altogether, it is a standard that I personally like because I think it would have a wholesome influence on human conduct. It may be that I like it because it would conduce to human welfare, so we are around in a circle again. I also rather like the standard of abundance and perfection of life which seems to have been the one favored by Darwin. Perhaps they both reduce to nearly or quite the same thing. But our conclusions as to whether they do or not, or how far they do, would depend upon the precise sense in which we used a lot of words, and on this topic I forbear to enter. If my intellectual bringing-up had been different, doubtless I would have preferred some other standard, since I might have been a Brahman or a strict Calvinist. So far as ethical theory is concerned, I am grateful for my bringing-up, and especially for having escaped Calvinism—which permits me to have a more human outlook on morals and enables me to contemplate my future destiny with a feeling of greater security.

CHAPTER IV

Natural Selection and the Evolution of Morals

> A tribe including many members who, from possessing in a high degree the spirit of patriotism, fidelity, obedience, courage, and sympathy were always ready to aid one another, and to sacrifice themselves for the common good, would be victorious over most other tribes.
> —CHARLES DARWIN, *The Descent of Man*

IN DISCUSSING THE PROBLEM of why man is moral I have, in a number of places, appealed to the operation of natural selection. To a very large extent morality, like religion, is obviously a product of cultural development. For this reason it might be inferred that natural selection could have had little to do with its evolution. The habit of muddling together the operations of biological and social forces is sometimes taken to be the besetting sin of the biologist who ventures to discuss the bearings of his science on social problems. It must be conceded that a number of early post-Darwinians were guilty of this fault to no small degree, and, although I shall endeavor to avoid falling into the same error, I can hardly expect to escape the reproach for so doing.

One often encounters such expressions as "the religious instinct," "the moral instinct," and even "the instinct against lying." But typically, instinct involves rather definite types of reactions to special objects or forces of the environment.

Variations in such actions, if they affect the likelihood of survival, may be readily conceived to accumulate and finally lead to more complex and better adapted forms of behavior. In the moral and religious conduct of human beings, however, acts are directed to countless different objects, when they are directed toward objects at all, and the kind of actions performed are dependent upon the products of thought. One could hardly explain the scrupulous honesty of the Igorrotes as contrasted with the mendacity of the Chipewyans as the direct result of differences in instinct. Nor is it reasonable to suppose that man is equipped with a specific instinct to be religious or just to be good any more than he could have evolved an instinct to become a plumber or a member of the Republican party. Nevertheless, in such acts as lying and stealing, and even in the conduct appropriate to the rôle of a plumber or a member of the Republican party, there are emotions involved which are associated with the basic instinctive drives common to all humanity. It is only these fundamental reaction patterns, with their accompanying emotions, that we can properly attribute to the action of biological selection in the strict sense. Being parts of our inherited make-up, these instincts and emotions present a problem that naturally comes within the province of biology. How these basic drives came to be woven into the complex fabric of human behavior patterns is, as we have so often been reminded, determined by man's experience with his environment.

This, if I understand him correctly, is the view of Darwin. Man, according to Darwin, has inherited an equipment of social instincts from his animal ancestors. "Although man as he now exists has few special instincts, having lost any which his early progenitors may have possessed, this is no reason why he should not have retained from an extremely remote period some degree of instinctive love and sympathy for his fellows." But Darwin is very careful not to appeal to instincts unduly, and certainly he would not now rank as a dyed-in-the-wool instinct psychologist, for he goes on to state: "We are indeed all conscious that we do possess such sympathetic feelings; but our consciousness does not tell us whether they are instinctive, having originated long ago in the same manner as with the lower animals, or whether they have been acquired by each of us during our early years. As man is a social animal, it is almost certain that he would inherit a tendency to be faithful to his comrades, and obedient to the leader of his tribe; for these qualities are common to most social animals . . . He would from an inherited tendency be willing to defend, in concert with others, his fellow men, and would be ready to aid them in any way, which did not too greatly interfere with his own welfare or his own strong desire." It is clear, I think, that Darwin held that man's endowment of social instincts is rather more meager than that of the animals from which he sprang, although man still retained a sufficient number of them to afford a sort of nucleus for the development of his moral sense. Man, Darwin believed, developed a consciousness of right and wrong because of his superior intellect that enables him to reflect upon the consequences of his actions. Animals do not possess a moral sense simply because they lack sufficient intelligence. With the proper endowment of social instincts, any animal, according to Darwin, "would inevitably acquire a moral sense, or conscience, as soon as its intellectual powers had become as well, or nearly as well developed as in man." According to Darwin, therefore, the part played by natural selection in making man inherently moral was to equip him, during the prehuman stages of his evolution, with useful social instincts and emotions with which, aided by his superior intelligence, he would be able to acquire a moral sense as a result of his experience with his fellows.

I have used the expression "inherently moral" advisedly, because I wish to point out that the process of selective survival has had effects upon man's cultural development quite aside from the accumulation of hereditary variations. There is constantly going on in society an elimination of individuals whose conduct evokes the disfavor of the group. This insubordination may not depend in the least upon any innate difference in the inherited constitution of the offender. But whatever the heredity of the individual may be, this elimination of the egregious helps to perpetuate the mores of the group and may even conduce to group survival. This kind of elimination Machin distinguishes by the term, "human selection." He points out its essential similarity to the process of artificial selection by which man improves his breeds of animals and plants, and he states, "Man as soon as he became social and obtained an intelligent grasp of his position, applied human selection also to the human members of his own society." Human selection is not, I think, necessarily, or even generally, "a conscious effort so to regulate social affairs that the society and its members may have the best chance of winning natural selection," because primitive man rarely acts with the deliberate intent of improving his group. In order to survive and leave offspring an individual must adjust himself to the mores of his society as he must adjust himself to his physical environment. If he fights an enemy and is killed, he is disposed of by natural selection because of his lack of strength or skill. If he violates a taboo and his tribesmen rise up in their wrath and put him to death, he suffers extinction because he failed to adjust himself to another aspect of his human environment. What the group approves tends to determine, in the long run, the kind of persons who survive and prosper. The effect of this selective process, like that of group selection, is to stimulate the development of bravery, reliability and cooperativeness, partly through the elimination of persons whose inborn traits do not favor the acquisition of these virtues, and partly also by strengthening the incentives that encourage their development in the individual.

The various forms of selection that influence the evolution of morals are closely interrelated in their action. Biological survival may conduce to the growth of an ideology, and conversely, an ideology may be an important aid to biological survival. A religion may spread extensively from its local source and supplant other religions with which it collides. Familiar examples are furnished by Christianity and Mohammedanism whose growth was rendered more rapid because persuasion was ably supplemented by the power of the sword. In these two instances the spread of the institution occurred largely through the incorporation of peoples of diverse nationality as well as by the rapid multiplication of their adherents. There are also many instances in which the expansion of a people is mainly due to its peculiar type of culture. A more highly civilized group may supplant more primitive peoples quite irrespective of its possibly superior inheritance. The Anglo-Saxons have increased enormously from a small band living around the mouth of the Elbe to a people of many millions controlling a large part of the surface of the globe, but their highly successful career was mainly the result of the military advantages conferred by their cultural development.

In the early periods of culture, when men were banded together in small clans and tribes, the moral customs that were followed were doubtless important factors in survival. The best moral practices tended to prevail because those who followed them increased more rapidly in numbers. This kind of institutional selection would tend to cause morals to be adjusted to the conditions under which people live. Through the preservation of variations in codes that favored biological survival, moral evolution might take place quite independently of any changes in the inherited constitutions of the peoples concerned. Even if all the tribes on a continent had exactly the same heredity, their morality might improve in adaptiveness as a result of selective survival. The transmission of favorable variations in conduct would occur through custom and tradition. In other words, social heredity would take the place of biological heredity as a means of perpetuating new modifications of behavior that proved to be useful. It is, I believe, to this kind of selection, however it may be designated, that the adaptiveness of moral codes is largely due.

There is also, as Professor S. Alexander has pointed out, a struggle of moral ideals, leading to the abandonment of those less suited to the conditions of the time. Ideals come to prevail because larger and larger numbers of individuals are persuaded to adopt them. In this process ideals spread, not through any relation to biological survival, but through their transmission from mind to mind. This kind of selective survival is, of course, analogous to natural selection, but there are no fatalities involved except to rejected ideals.

The application of natural selection in the field of morals has evoked much criticism. Although the rôle of group selection as well as individual selection has generally been recognized, one rarely meets with any adequate comprehension of the varied ways in which selection affects the development of moral conduct. So far as my acquaintance goes, the most extensive list of the different modes in which selection operates is that of J. Mark Baldwin, who distinguishes fourteen in all, but not nearly all of them are relevant to our theme. (See *Development and Evolution,* p. 166.) The types I have mentioned include, I think, the most important of the selective activities concerned in the evolution of morals.

CHAPTER V

Evolutionary Theories of Conscience

> The conscience is the utterance of the public spirit of the race, ordering us to obey the primary conditions of its welfare, and it acts not the less forcibly though we may not understand the source of its authority or the end at which it is aiming.
> —LESLIE STEPHEN, *The Science of Ethics*

ANYONE WHO ADOPTS a naturalistic ethics faces the challenge of the problem of conscience. What kind of answers can he give to the questions: What is the nature of this inner voice? With what authority does it speak? How did this peculiar faculty come to exist in us? There are many diverse opinions as to what the possession of a conscience implies. According to some moralists it implies much, even affording, as was maintained by Kant, the grounds for belief in God, the freedom of the will, and the immortality of the soul. For other moralists conscience has no more significance for metaphysics or theology than our feelings of sympathy, pride, or any other elements of our conscious experience.

According to a traditional and widespread view, conscience is a faculty with which man is endowed to enable him to distinguish between right and wrong, and which urges him to follow the one and abstain from the other. As expressed by Bishop Butler, "this faculty was placed within to be our proper governor; to direct and regulate all under-principles, passions, and motives of action. This is its right and office; thus sacred is its authority. And how often soever men violate and rebelliously refuse to submit to it, for supposed interest which they cannot otherwise obtain, or for the sake of passion which they cannot otherwise gratify; this makes no alteration as to the natural right and office of conscience."

From this standpoint conscience affords a kind of divine revelation concerning right and wrong. But observation of the actual workings of this faculty fails to justify the high claims that are often made for it. It is frequently unreasonable and inconsistent in its promptings and is far from being an infallible guide to right conduct, unless, of course, we define right conduct as that which conscience approves. People have burned witches and tortured heretics in obedience to the most conscientious of motives. What the conscience of people approves or disapproves depends to a large extent upon education and the traditional mores of the group from which their moral standards have been derived. Under just the right kind of discipline it might be made to approve of almost any kind of iniquity.

While numerous Christian moralists have interpreted conscience as a supernatural endowment whose position in our nature, as expressed by Lecky, "is wholly unique," writers of a rationalistic bent have endeavored to analyze it in terms of sympathy, benevolence, pride, shame, and other emotions and sentiments. Bentham and J. S. Mill interpreted conscience as resulting from experiences of the pleasures or pains associated with certain acts. Speaking of virtue, Mr. Mill in his essay on *Utilitarianism* states, "There was no original desire for it, or motive to it, save its conduciveness to pleasure and especially to protection from pain. But through the association thus formed it may be felt a good in itself, and desired as such with as great intensity as any other good." Our love of virtue and hatred of evil are therefore acquired tastes. Conscience says, in effect, to its possessor, 'Follow me; I am the voice of experience, and what I tell you to do and not to do will bring you happiness and freedom from pain.'"

The associationist psychology continued to influence the thinking of writers on evolutionary ethics as is conspicuously illustrated by Herbert Spencer, to whose treatment of the moral sense we now turn. Mr. Spencer was an adherent of the so-called experience philosophy, but in his psychology and ethics he appeals not so much to individual experience as to ancestral experience whose effects were supposed to be accumulated through hereditary transmission during countless ages. Our emotions and our intuitions of space and time, which appear to be innate and *a priori* in the individual, are interpreted as derived from the accumulated effects of environmental contacts. In a letter to Mill, Spencer stated his view "that, corresponding to the fundamental conception of a developed 'Moral Science,' there have been, and still are developing in the race, certain fundamental moral intuitions; and that, though these intuitions are the results of accumulated experiences of utility, gradually organized and inherited, they have come to be quite independent of conscious experience."

Conscience thus speaks with the wisdom derived from experience, but from experience immeasurably longer than any individual life. This extension of the experience philosophy, upon which Mr. Spencer seems to have especially prided himself, suffers from the drawback of being founded upon the Lamarckian doctrine of the transmission of acquired characters which is now generally discarded by biologists. No reader of Spencer's *Principles of Psychology* can fail to note how extensively the author has built upon Lamarckian foundations in that very original and able work.

Many ingenious explanations in Spencer's volumes on biology, psychology, sociology and ethics will have to stand or fall with the fate of the Lamarckian theory. Although Lamarckism has never been defended with greater ability, even by its devotees among professional biologists, there can be little doubt that the verdict of history will be that Spencer was fighting for a lost cause.

The writings of Charles Darwin on ethics differ strikingly from those of Spencer. The ethical doctrines of these great leaders of evolutionary thought were to a large extent independently developed, but although Spencer had elaborated many features of his ethical philosophy before the Darwinian theory was promulgated, Darwin probably owed less to Spencer than Spencer owed to Darwin. The widest divergence in the ethical views of these writers is found in their derivation of conscience. According to both authors conscience is a derivative faculty based on feelings and emotions having their roots in our remote animal ancestry. Spencer held that these feelings and emotions are highly complex psychical states slowly built up through successive generations. Their apparent simplicity is quite deceptive. As an illustration of their complex nature Spencer refers to the feelings aroused by contemplating a beautiful landscape. These feelings include not merely the sensations immediately aroused, but "the myriads of sensations that have been in times past received from objects such as those presented," and in addition, "there are partially excited the multitudinous incidental feelings that were experienced on those many past occasions; and there are also excited certain deeper, but more vague combinations of states which were organized in the race during barbaric times, when its pleasurable activities were chiefly among the woods and waters." According to Spencer, therefore, our emotions are fearfully and wonderfully made. And especially the higher emotions associated with moral conduct must be compounds of almost unimaginable complexity.

Neither in *The Descent of Man* nor in his volume on *The Expression of the Emotions in Man and Animals* does one find any indication that Darwin believed that emotions are highly compounded states. Apparently he regarded them as relatively simple, psychologically, and intimately associated with instinct. He held that our instincts and their accompanying emotions constitute the basis of our conscience, or moral sense, but while Spencer appealed mainly to the Lamarckian factor in building up the emotional components of this faculty, Darwin attributed its origin, in so far as it is based on impulses, chiefly to natural selection. Aside from the fact that both accounts of conscience are naturalistic and evolutionary, their divergence is wide.

Darwin's position is best stated in his own words.

"Any animal whatever, endowed with well marked social instincts, the parental and filial affections being here included, would inevitably acquire a moral sense or conscience, as soon as its intellectual powers had become as well, or nearly as well developed, as in man. For, firstly, the social instincts lead an animal to take pleasure in the society of its fellows, to feel a certain amount of sympathy with them and to perform various services for them. Secondly, as soon as the mental faculties had become highly developed, images of all past actions and motives would be incessantly passing through the brain of each individual; and that feeling of dissatisfaction, or even misery, which invariably results, as we shall hereafter see, from any unsatisfied instinct, would arise, as often as it was perceived that the enduring and always present social instinct had yielded to some other instinct, at the time stronger but neither enduring in its nature, nor leaving behind it a very vivid impression. Thirdly, after the power of language had been acquired, and the wishes of the community could be expressed, the common opinion how each member ought to act for the public good would naturally become in a paramount degree the guide to action. But it should be borne in mind that, however great weight we may attribute to public opinion, our regard for the approbation and disapprobation of our fellows depends on sympathy, which, as we shall see, forms an essential part of the social instinct, and is indeed as its foundation-stone. Lastly, habit in the individual would ultimately play a very important part in guiding the conduct of each member; for the social instinct, together with sympathy, is, like any other instinct, greatly strengthened by habit, and so consequently would be obedience to the wishes and judgment of the community."

Darwin then proceeds to elaborate these several points. Social animals, he points out, perform many services to their mutual advantage, such as posting sentinels, making warning cries, mutual feeding, ministration to sick members of the group, and cooperating in the defense of attacked comrades. The gregarious propensities and social instincts and affections of animals which lead to so many unselfish acts are attributed by Darwin in part to habit, but chiefly to natural selection. "With those animals which were benefited by living in close association," he says, "the individuals which took the greatest pleasure in society would best escape various dangers, whilst those that cared least for their comrades, and lived solitary, would perish in greater numbers. With respect to the origin of the parental and filial affections, which apparently lie at the base of the social instincts, we know not the steps by which they have been gained; but we may infer that it has been to a large extent through natural selection."

Instinctive sympathy, which plays an important rôle in

the higher social and gregarious animals, would tend to be intensified by natural selection wherever advantageous to the group. Although Darwin believed that man has lost several instincts of his quadrumanous ancestors, he held that the germs at least of a number of them are retained, and these through education and habit tend to fit man to be a truly social animal. "Instinctive sympathy would also cause him to value highly the approbation of his fellows; for, as Mr. Bain has clearly shown, the love of praise and the strong feeling of glory, and the still stronger horror of scorn and infamy, 'are due to the workings of sympathy.' Consequently man would be influenced in the highest degree by the wishes, approbation, and blame of his fellow-men, as expressed by their gestures and language. Thus the social instincts, which must have been acquired by man in a very rude state, and probably even by his early ape-like progenitors, still give the impulse to some of his best actions; but his actions are in a higher degree determined by the expressed wishes and judgment of his fellow-men, and unfortunately very often by his own strong selfish desires. But as love, sympathy and self-command become strengthened by habit, and as the power of reasoning becomes clearer, so that man can value justly the judgments of his fellows, he will feel himself impelled, apart from any transitory pleasure or pain, to certain lines of conduct."

And now comes a conclusion to which Darwin attached great weight, "the main point, on which, from our present point of view, the whole question of the moral sense turns." "Why," asks Darwin, "should a man feel that he ought to obey one instinctive desire rather than another? Why is he bitterly regretful, if he has yielded to a strong sense of self-preservation, and has not risked his life to save that of a fellow-creature? Or why does he regret having stolen food from hunger?" Sometimes the unselfish impulse is followed because it is the stronger, as in the individual who, "full of courage and sympathy, has disregarded the instinct of self-preservation and plunged at once into a torrent to save a drowning man, though a stranger." But these impulsive acts are exceptional and do not explain the deliberate choice of the better way when one can weigh the probable effects of alternative courses of action. "It is untenable," Darwin concedes, "that in man the social instincts (including the love of praise and fear of blame) possess greater strength, or have, through long habit, acquired greater strength than the instincts of self-preservation, hunger, lust, vengeance, etc. Why then does man regret, even though trying to banish such regret, that he has followed the one natural impulse rather than the other?"

Here is Darwin's answer:

"A man cannot prevent past impressions often repassing through his mind; he will thus be driven to make a comparison between the impressions of past hunger, vengeance satisfied, or danger shunned at other men's cost, with the almost ever-present instinct of sympathy, and with his early knowledge of what others consider as praiseworthy or blamable. This knowledge cannot be banished from his mind, and from instinctive sympathy is esteemed of great moment. He will then feel as if he had been baulked in following a present instinct or habit, and this with all animals causes dissatisfaction, or even misery. . . .

"At the moment of action, man will no doubt be apt to follow the stronger impulse; and though this may occasionally prompt him to the noblest deeds, it will more commonly lead him to gratify his own desires at the expense of other men. But after their gratification, when past and weaker impressions are judged by the ever-enduring social instinct, and by his deep regard for the good opinion of his fellows, retribution will surely come. He will then feel remorse, repentance, regret, or shame; this latter feeling, however, relates almost exclusively to the judgment of others. He will consequently resolve more or less firmly to act differently for the future; and this is conscience; for conscience looks backwards, and serves as a guide for the future."

A very important element of the moral sense is the value man places on the approbation of his fellows and his dread of their disapproval. Added to these are the reverence for and fear of gods and spirits. A case in point is afforded by the Australian native who lost his wife and told the magistrate that he was going to a distant tribe to spear another woman in satisfaction for his loss, this being the approved procedure in such matters among the natives of Western Australia. The magistrate threatened him with severe punishment if he carried out his intent. But the poor savage became restless, complained that he could not eat or sleep, grew thin, and said that his wife's spirit was haunting him for not properly avenging her death. Finally he disappeared. After more than a year's absence, he returned in good condition and in a peaceful and satisfied frame of mind and with no more qualms of conscience. He had killed his woman. His categorical imperative had spoken and he had obeyed. The sweet peace of duty performed had come into his soul.

For us, brought up under the influence of very different conceptions of right conduct, it is difficult to understand how the willful and premeditated murder of a stranger, who had never done the savage the least harm, could have been committed with the most conscientious motives. But the savage was simply following a tribal custom supported by the strongest of sanctions. If he failed to follow the prescribed course he would be disgraced in the eyes of his tribe, his gods, and the spirit of his departed wife.

Tribal customs and taboos hold the savage in an iron grip.

Conformity constitutes the great moral principle of his life. When he does what is expected of him his conscience is satisfied. To a large extent this is true of the rest of us. This fact is illustrated, as Darwin pointed out, by the so-called law of honor, which is based upon the opinions and sentiments of the class to which one belongs. A breach of the code of honor may fill one with a profound sense of shame and humiliation. Even a violation of a rule of etiquette may excite feelings of regret and wounded pride that are closely akin to the prickings of the guilty conscience. From the Darwinian viewpoint conscience cannot be looked upon as a single faculty which a phrenologist conceivably might locate in a bump in the head; rather it is a psychological complex of varied elements intellectual and emotional. Fear, shame, anger, sympathy, affection, pride, humiliation, regret, and other emotions and sentiments may, at different times and in different proportions, enter into its functioning according to the circumstances of the individual case. The moral sense is a name for a group of judgments and emotions in relation to the valuation of behavior. Darwin's account of it, purely as a matter of psychological analysis, is a marked improvement over that of his predecessors. Yet I cannot help thinking that he has overstressed the importance of duration in causing a higher value to be set upon the social than the self-regarding impulses. In this he has laid himself open to a criticism which has been urged with especial force by President J. G. Schurman in his volume on *The Ethical Import of Darwinism*. This work is one of the ablest and on the whole fairest criticisms of Darwinian ethics, and forms a striking contrast to most of the diatribes that followed upon the publication of *The Descent of Man*. Written by a philosopher of the intuitionist school strongly influenced by the teachings of Kant, Schurman's criticisms are based upon an ethical viewpoint fundamentally at variance with that of Darwin. The author expresses "indebtedness to Darwin" whose ethical speculations he has found "more stimulating than any other work since the time of Kant." He emphasizes the importance of the theory of evolution in the study of the moral life, but he holds, in common with many other philosophers, that the really fundamental problems of ethics are little affected by this theory. The main brunt of his attack is directed against the Darwinian theory of the origin of the moral sense, and it will be instructive to consider briefly some of his chief objections.

Commenting on Darwin's contention that the moral supremacy of the unselfish instincts is due to their greater permanence, Dr. Schurman in the first place denies the generality of this alleged fact. Only some social instincts are more permanent than some egoistic ones. "The instinct of self-preservation," he observes, "comes earliest; and as the filial, parental and social instincts are derived from it by means of natural selection, there would be grounds for maintaining that the one omnipresent and persistent impulse is the egoistic one of self-preservation."

And besides, "You cannot argue that because selfish impulses do not come so often or stay so long as the social impulses, they have therefore less right to the field when they actually do put in an appearance. Granting that the times of sociability are greater than the times of selfishness, this time measure does not explain why I feel remorse over acts of vengeance and robbery. . . . Reflection, then, will not generate remorse in a being that recognizes no differences in impulses to action except degrees of duration and intensity." The evolutionist, according to Schurman, is continually trying to derive moral sentiments out of experiences that really presuppose them; and hence he really begs the entire question at issue.

It must be conceded, I think, that Darwin's interpretation

of the particular point discussed is open to the objection that Schurman has urged against it, but the whole case of the Darwinian does not hinge upon this issue. It is not so much the persistence of the social impulses, as their quality, that gives them their moral significance. But Schurman's more fundamental contention that the Darwinian argument begs the question applies no more to the evolution of conscience than to the evolution of anything else. The component elements of conscience are inevitably presupposed in any evolutionary derivation of this faculty. Even if we grant that the moral sense is a unique endowment of man, one does not argue in a circle by assuming that its bases are found in our subhuman ancestors. The ingredients of a cake are presupposed in accounting for the finished product, but the ingredients are not the cake. In his endeavor to show that his doctrine of descent is consistent with all the facts, Darwin attempted to show that, given a creature with the capacity for feeling sympathy, affection, pride, shame, and other emotions that man shares with the higher mammals, and having the additional endowment of reason and the ability to reflect upon the consequences of actions, a moral sense would naturally arise. To such a derivation Schurman was fundamentally opposed. He was committed to a sort of mystical conception of conscience as a faculty whose origin cannot be explained. It is just based on a moral intuition of the mind. He grandiloquently speaks of "our sense of an absolutely worthful, the right, not merely the useful, and our recognition of its authority over us as expressed in the word 'ought.'" For these ideas, he tells us, "no experience can account."

In reading Dr. Schurman's volume one catches the spirit of the old-time controversies between science and theology. On the one hand we have the desire for explanation and the dissipation of mystery; on the other the tendency to take refuge in something that science cannot fathom and which compels us to have recourse to God or some transcendental principle of metaphysics. This essentially theological attitude hangs on in ethics after it is practically abandoned almost everywhere else. Conscience has long been and still is its chief stronghold.

A valuable supplement to Darwin's theory of conscience was supplied by W. K. Clifford in his able essay on *The Scientific Basis of Morals*. As might have been expected from a person of his keen, original and scientifically trained mind, Clifford departed from the traditional expositions of ethics and enriched the literature of the subject with a fresh and vigorous treatment which has elicited widespread commendation. Conscience, according to Clifford, has been developed from the notion of the tribal self. The idea is of course analogous to that of the individual or personal self, but individuals identify themselves more in primitive than in advanced societies with the tribe, or group to which they belong. "The savage is not only hurt when anybody treads on his foot, but when anybody treads on his tribe." The thought of how his acts will appear in the eyes of his associates is ever before his mind. "Now suppose," says Clifford, "that a man has done something obviously harmful to the community. Either some immediate desire, or his individual self, has for once proved stronger than the tribal self. When the tribal self wakes up, the man says 'in the name of the tribe, I do not like this thing that I, as an individual, have done.' This self judgment in the name of the tribe is called Conscience. If a man goes further and draws from this act and others an inference about his own character, he may say, 'in the name of the tribe, I do not like my individual self.' This is remorse."

According to Clifford the sense of solidarity, which the notion of the tribal self tends to intensify, will be strengthened by natural selection. The individual comes habitually to think the maxim, "'Put yourself in his place." His love of the approbation of his fellows, his pride in receiving their commendation, and the thought of how they might feel and act if he violated the code of the tribe, produce a habitual conformity to the voice of the tribal self. And the thought of spirits who can see him when no one else is near and who can visit their displeasure in ways that he is powerless to avoid, affords a powerful additional motive to conformity.

Social disapproval is a very unpleasant experience for any normal person, and the very thought of it causes a certain amount of self-reproach. The desire to stand well in one's own estimation, which is evidently a derived sentiment, would probably never arise in us if we did not habitually think how we might stand in the estimation of others. Being social animals, we want to meet the approval of our fellows. Even if we knew that an offense could never be found out, we could not suppress something of the same kind of social dread that would arise if it became known.

Conscience, therefore, is essentially social in origin. As T. H. Green remarks, "No individual can make a conscience for himself. He always needs a society to make it for him." But it has been truly stated that conscience sometimes prompts a man to follow a course of action that will bring upon him the reproaches of all his fellows. In the solitary grandeur of his own high ideal of what is right, a man may defy the disapproval and even the punishment he would incur in being true to himself. He may do this even if he is an atheist and deprived of the martyr's consolation of being alone with God. Nevertheless the sympathy, love of kind, pride, or other impulses, which may have motivated his conduct, would never have been a part of his nature did he not belong to a species whose members are adapted to group life. In a person with a highly developed power of reflective thought and habituated to critical and independent cogitation on all sorts of problems, one may expect almost any kind of conclusion as to specific duties. If his judgment told him that an act is right, his sense of justice and his regard for the general welfare would urge him to perform it. After all, he would really be obeying the voice of the group.

CHAPTER VI

Human Nature in the Light of Darwinism

> Man is explicable by nothing less than all his history.—EMERSON

IF ONE IS AN ORTHODOX Darwinian, certain general outlines of his conception of human nature are thereby cut out for him. Looking upon man as having been evolved from lower forms of animal life through the operation of natural selection, he must conclude that all the native traits of human nature, not of fortuitous origin, owe their presence, directly or indirectly, to selective survival. If we ask, therefore, concerning the reasons why we possess any of our native endowments, the answer must be that it is owing to their value in the struggle for existence. A simple explanation, no doubt, so far as it goes. But even if it does not take us very far toward a complete analysis, its consequences are very far reaching and revolutionary.

The Darwinian interpretation, which makes man a part and parcel of nature in all aspects of his being, represents an important attempt to attain a true scientific understanding in a field long obscured by the clouds of mystery. Pre-evolutionary efforts to give a naturalistic account of man suffered from a fearful handicap. The intrepid spirits who essayed the task, such as the materialistic philosophers of the eighteenth century, had no adequate way of meeting the old argument from design so forcibly elaborated later by William Paley.

All their argumentations seemed only to emphasize the futility of their aim.

For ages man has been looked upon as a sort of meeting ground of natural and supernatural forces. Predominant interest was centered on the fact that human nature includes both good and evil propensities in proportions that vary greatly in different individuals. A few of them are truly sublime souls, while others are miserable wretches who seem to be the incarnation of everything that is vile. A number of theories to account for this situation are based upon the assumption of eternal principles of good and evil which may have their personal embodiment in good or evil supernatural beings, with man occupying the unfortunate position of a bone of contention between the opposed forces. Ormuzd and Ahriman, Yang and Yin, God and Satan, strive for mastery, and now good and now evil prevails, depending upon the relative success of the contending powers. According to Hebrew and Christian tradition, all of our woe was brought into the world by man's first disobedience. After the fatal episode of the forbidden fruit when, "In Adam's fall sinned we all," man has suffered from the effects of original sin. His nature became corrupted and, according to some high theological authorities, even totally depraved and deserving of eternal damnation. Devils, witches, and maleficent spirits of all sorts who, through the mysterious dispensation of Providence, were permitted to continue their depredations, constantly harassed mankind, brought upon them all sorts of misfortunes, and led multitudes to follow evil ways. So poor man suffered, not only from his own proper infirmities resulting from original sin, but also from numerous other afflictions arising from the continued machinations of evil spirits.

Such were the conceptions of man and his place in the universe that prevailed during most of the Christian era.

The human suffering inflicted as a logical consequence of these conceptions surpasses our powers of description. But after the decline of the belief in witchcraft and demoniacal possession, the old animistic conceptions of human nature continued to persist, and they are still widely prevalent. Even in the days of witchcraft a great deal had been learned about human nature through simple observation and reflection. Granting that man was miraculously created, there is, of course, much concerning the organization and the development of his mind that can be scientifically explained. Following the Schoolmen, who endeavored to secure some rational understanding of the workings of the intellect, Bacon, Descartes, Hobbes, Locke, Spinoza, Hartley, Berkeley, Hume, and later students of the operations of the mind, made substantial contributions to the science of psychology; but to the question as to why human nature is constituted as it is, they gave no satisfactory answer.

The first serious attempts to explain human nature as a product of organic evolution were made by Lamarck, and more explicitly by Herbert Spencer. In both of these attempts the inherited effects of experience were appealed to as the chief factor of evolutionary change. For this reason they both suffer from basing their derivations upon a probably false doctrine. But even if the so-called Lamarckian factor is a *vera causa* of the transformation of species, it is incapable of explaining many features of mental development. Darwin's theory of natural selection proved to be a much more fruitful principle of explanation.

Quite naturally it was the application of this doctrine to explain the evolution of the mental powers and moral impulses of man that aroused the most vigorous opposition. Darwin's loyal supporter and co-discoverer of the principle of natural selection, Alfred Russel Wallace, who was even more of a selectionist than Darwin himself when it came to most biological problems, balked at applying the doctrine to the evolution of man's higher faculties. Hence nothing short of a miraculous intervention would do to account for the distinctive qualities of man's mind. Many adherents of the Roman Catholic Church, who accept the doctrine of evolution as applied to the animal world, and even to the human body, hold that the human soul is the product of a special creation. In conceding evolution to this extent, they have gone as far as the fundamentals of their faith permit.

As interpreted according to the Darwinian Theory, human nature inevitably appears in a light very different from that in which it was formerly regarded. Even our slight frown of annoyance has its evolutionary significance in terms of past utilities. Darwin's book on *The Expression of the Emotions in Man and Animals* brings out in a most striking manner numerous close similarities in emotion and emotional expression in man and the higher mammals, and interprets many of these in terms of instinctive activities. Our bodily expression of anger, for instance: the tense muscles, the quickened heartbeat and respiration, the expanded nostrils, the fixed gaze, the frown that shades the eyes, and the muscular contraction that produces our vestigial manifestation of snarling, not only betray our kinship with the higher mammals, but they are reactions that aid in preparing the body for fighting. The later investigations of Cannon have revealed parallel internal changes which cooperate to the same end. In anger there is a greater output of sugar in the blood, supplying energy for muscular contraction, greater secretion of adrenin which stimulates muscular contractility, a diversion of blood from the viscera to the brain and the muscles, and a more rapid consumption of oxygen. These internal physiological changes mobilize the energies of the body for conflict. Their biological significance is essentially like that of the accompanying external signs of anger described by Darwin. They all have their meaning in relation to survival.

Following the work of Darwin there have been many attempts to interpret the biological significance of the various character traits of human beings. The psychological standpoint of the Darwinian is much like that of the comparative physiologist who endeavors to show how the various activities of the organism conduce to the maintenance of the life of the whole, and to ascertain the stages by which the several functions came to be evolved. The question which the Darwinian is prone to ask, first of all, concerning fear, anger, pride, shame, sympathy, and other parts of our psychological make-up is, What is its functional significance in the maintenance and perpetuation of life? In some cases a plausible answer is fairly easy; in others one can offer only a rather unsatisfactory guess. In any case, however, it may be helpful to consider briefly a few of our human character traits from this evolutionary viewpoint.

FEAR

That fear is one of the primary emotions of man is conceded even by most opponents of the "instinct psychology," who try to avoid attributing anything to instinct if they can possibly get out of it. We all know what fear feels like, although it is not safe to assume that animals which manifest fear have the same conscious states that we have. Nothing evokes the protest of a comparative psychologist so quickly as our common habit of what Wasmann calls, "humanizing the brute," or interpreting animal behavior in terms of our own conscious experience. This is especially dangerous in regard to primitive forms of life. A lot of cockroaches or fiddler crabs will scuttle away in apparent alarm at one's approach, but what kind of conscious states these creatures have is known only to the animals themselves. Instincts to escape from danger go far down in the animal kingdom. They may lead, as they commonly do, to flight; they may impel an animal to hide, or they may cause it to become immobile and thus more likely to escape detection. Fear as manifested by most animals, and especially in man, is a generalized instinct. It is often evoked by loud, unusual sounds or large and strange, moving objects. As a boy on a farm I often amused myself by throwing my hat in the air and enjoying the consternation in the poultry yard. The chickens reacted to the hat much as they do to the flight of a hawk, and often gave the same note of alarm. Hudson, in his excellent observations on fear in birds, has found that fear becomes attached to specific objects as a result of experience and tradition. Birds come to fear creatures that elicit notes of alarm or other signs of fear in other birds, so that their original, ill defined fear instinct becomes conditioned in relation to particular enemies. It is much the same with all higher animals. The human infant is especially prone to be startled by loud noises; later, fears come to be associated with specific objects such as snakes, spiders, dogs, and even imaginary objects such as ghosts. Personally I do not have the slightest belief in ghosts, but I have been conditioned to fear them from having heard ghost stories early in life. If I were alone at night in a haunted house, I am sure that I could not entirely suppress the peculiar uncanny feeling that ghost stories formerly aroused.

A large part of the fears that people exhibit are quite foolish. Many a woman has stood up on a chair and called wildly for help because she saw a poor little mouse running on the floor. The recognition that a fear is unreasonable is often quite powerless to expel it. A child may be frightened by a person wearing a hideous mask, although he may have seen the mask put on. The fear instinct asserts itself in plain defiance of knowledge and reason. Under present conditions of civilization many fear reactions certainly serve no useful function. This is to be expected on account of the general and undefined nature of the original fear impulse, and the fact that fears are so readily conditioned in early periods of life.

Many of these fears are instilled into the child by his associates. Once acquired they may be intensified by habit, especially if the fear is shared by others. The modern child, living a protected life, is no longer exposed to several dangers that were encountered in more primitive times. Ferocious beasts are rarely seen except in cages, and strangers are not apt to be dangerous. A young child may fear strangers nevertheless, as an infant is sometimes terrorized at the first sight of a cat or a dog. Fear of the unknown is a basic trait of animal and man alike and, on the whole, it is a very useful endowment. It means playing safe. If I should meet with a gorilla in the wilds of Africa, I should take care that he did not come too close to me, knowing that he could easily break every bone in my body. The gorilla, being a retiring animal by nature, would probably act on the same principle, since the sight of me would doubtless send him scuttling away through the forest. There is scarcely a higher animal, however powerful, whose life is free from the fear of ever-possible dangers. No wonder, therefore, that this instinct is deeply ingrained in our constitution and is at times capable of taking a powerful hold upon us, overmastering our reason and even paralyzing our energies. We can never shake ourselves free from the fear of the unknown and we should not. With man and animal alike the promptings of instinct coincide with the voice of wisdom.

It is a familiar fact that fear may be aroused in the absence of any threatening object by situations which may entail lack of security. Man, being a gregarious animal, is often afflicted with fear of solitude. Children are commonly afraid of being left alone in the dark, and their fear may be greatly intensified if they have been told spooky stories. The vague general dread of some unknown danger, or of some dreadful creature that might come in the stillness of the night when no one is near, is promptly stilled by the reassuring presence of well-known associates. The fear of open spaces (agoraphobia), which in certain people amounts to an obsession, is an allied feeling which is evinced by many animals having a strong instinct to keep close to shelter. The opposite fear of being confined (claustrophobia) is exhibited very frequently by animals, and has its very obvious utility for all animals that are preyed upon.

Occasions that justify primitive fear reactions have become less frequent as man has advanced, but social fears of various kinds come to play a prominent rôle. There is a fear of disapproval, of ridicule, of gods, of ghosts, and other members of an imaginary social world to which adjustments have to be made. The world of supernatural beings is very real to the savage. If he violates a tribal taboo, if he displeases the spirit of a departed relative or friend, or incurs the wrath of some powerful divinity, he may suffer all sorts of dire misfortunes. To a large extent primitive religion is based on fear. Doubtless this fear of the supernatural has been a useful force in controlling conduct in the interest of tribal welfare. But the benefits thus obtained were purchased at the price of ages of terror.

The rôle of fear in human conduct is by no means limited to the functioning of this emotion as such. Fear enters as a component into several sentiments which have a profound influence upon human behavior, as has been clearly brought out by Shand in his valuable work on *The Foundations of Character*. Jealousy, awe, anxiety, and reverence are complex states in which fear enters as one factor in the blend of emotions. The number of states that we class under these names may be very great, depending upon the relative rôles played by the component emotions and the varied intellectual elements associated with them.

ANGER AND THE INSTINCT OF PUGNACITY

Anger, like fear, is one of the basic human emotions and its normal concomitant, the fighting instinct, like the instincts of flight and concealment, had its beginnings far down in the animal kingdom. Behavior antagonistic to that of another animal does not necessarily imply anger. The activities of overcoming prey long preceded the advent of pugnacity properly so-called. A jellyfish or a starfish may struggle to capture and devour another animal, but no one would think of attributing the emotion of anger to animals so low in the scale. Lions and tigers make use of claws and teeth in the normal process of food-getting, and the same equipment is employed in a more or less similar fashion in fights with their enemies. Many structures which were evolved primarily for the function of securing food were worked in later in the service of true pugnacity. Doubtless also, the instincts employed in dealing with prey found an additional usefulness, in a modified form, in dealing with rivals. It would be a great error, however, to attempt to derive the fighting propensities from the instincts of food-getting. Many kinds of herbivorous animals are highly pugnacious and have become equipped with horns and other weapons having the obvious function of inflicting damage upon their enemies.

The one cause that arouses the fighting propensities is some kind of interference. So long as a creature has everything its own way it rarely makes trouble. But if one dog attempts to share another dog's bone, or if one child grabs a plaything from another child, or if the natural inclination of an animal is thwarted in any way, there is resentment and resistance. Consider for a moment the things that animals fight about. There is first of all food, or it may be the occupation of a particular habitat. Then there are the battles of males for the possession of the females, which have been described in detail in Darwin's writings on sexual selection. The prevalence of horns, tusks, protective manes, spurs, and the large size and strength of many male animals is an impressive testimony of the extent of this kind of rivalry. The large male sea lion fights away all smaller males and surrounds himself with as many females as he can appropriate. Younger males may hang longingly at safe distance around the outskirts of the herd in the hope of enticing a female to leave the circle of the tyrant. Sometimes a female who is the bone of contention between two rival males is literally torn to pieces in the efforts to possess her. Among birds there are battles to prevent interference with the processes of rearing young, and in social animals there are battles for the protection of the group.

The occasions for anger in man are much the same fundamentally as in animals, although they are increased by the multitude of interests which result from the greater activities of human intelligence. Prominent among the causes of anger among human beings are acts which reduce what psychologists call our positive self-feeling. Insults, sneers, ridicule, and being snubbed or disregarded as a being of no consequence may arouse intense resentment and in former times led to frequent duels. It is only in the most highly developed among the lower animals, and more especially in the apes, that such offenses against personal dignity have the least effect. Laughter or mockery may throw a chimpanzee into a violent rage, but a cat or a dog would not be capable of interpreting such acts as a personal affront. In the old dueling days men were very touchy about their honor; anything that detracted from it was a deprivation more keenly felt than a loss of money or a physical injury. Honor was the one thing that a gentleman could not permit to be interfered with. With Cyrano or one of Dumas's Musketeers, the least innuendo, or a semblance of a rude stare might provoke a challenge.

From the standpoint of the evolution of morals the most important feature of man's fighting instinct is his group pugnacity. On the whole, man is probably more warlike than his subhuman ancestors. For untold ages clan has fought with clan and tribe with tribe. Hence man has been subject to a process of group selection which has tended to develop the instincts that have made for effective cooperation. His nature has been molded by strife and for strife. Speaking of the conflicts of the headhunters of Borneo, whom he describes as "very intelligent, and sociable and kindly to one another within each village community," McDougall remarks, "This perpetual warfare, like the squabbles of a room full of quarrelsome children, seems to be almost wholly and directly due to the uncomplicated operation of the instinct of pugnacity. No material benefits are sought; a few heads and sometimes a slave or two are the only trophies gained; and, if one asks of an intelligent chief why he keeps up this senseless practice of going on the war path, the best reason he can give is that unless he does so his neighbors will not respect him and his people, and will fall upon them and exterminate them."

From the time of the earliest written records literature has celebrated the glories of war. The *Iliad*, the *Odyssey*, the *Aeneid*, the epics of the Norsemen and even *Paradise Lost* have extolled the exploits of conquering heroes, and most histories recount with pride the victories and justify the wars of the nations to which the historian happened to belong. Deeply imbedded in our human nature is the impulse to do battle, to lay about one lustily, and to engage in the wanton destruction of the possessions of the enemy. Provoked by interference, anger is directed to getting rid of interference by destroying, disabling, or driving away the offender. It is just one of the several manifestations of the will to live.

As in the case of fear, the emotion of anger plays a useful part as a component of more complex sentiments which exert a continual influence on our everyday conduct. Jealously, rivalry, emulation, contempt, righteous indignation, and even the grim determination to overcome obstacles, are complex states into which pugnacity enters as an important element. A little spice of it seasons many of our sentiments and impulses. Tempered and controlled and harnessed to the service of our higher aims, this emotion contributes greatly to the effectiveness of our lives. Try to imagine Theodore Roosevelt without his bump of combativeness and you will picture a very different and much less forceful personality. A mollycoddle, doubtless, to use one of his own expressions. Cooley has well said, "Life without opposition is Capua. No matter what the part one is fitted to play in it, he can make progress in his path only by a vigorous assault upon the obstacles, and to be vigorous the assault must be supported by passion of some sort. With most of us the requisite intensity of passion is not forthcoming without an element of resentment; and common sense and careful observation will, I believe, confirm the opinion that few people who amount to much are without a good capacity for hostile feelings, upon which they can draw freely when they need it." And Dr. George Stratton states that, "Anger . . . is not a purely negative, a destructive energy. It joins in the great work of upbuilding. . . . we owe much of our social life within the state to indignation, resentment, jealousy and revenge. . . . They have been the strength and defense of this whole fabric of rights and duties." We should doubtless feel grateful for the fact that our animal ancestors tore one another with tooth and claw. Without this struggle we would never have become human.

JEALOUSY

Although jealousy is not a simple emotion, it affords an instructive illustration of the extent to which our character traits reach far down in the animal kingdom. George Romanes describes a cockatoo which flew in rage at a small green parrot when it was stroked by its mistress. Everyone has observed jealousy in dogs. It may be very intense in monkeys. Miss Romanes, in describing the jealous behavior of a pet Cebus monkey that was very fond of her mother, relates that when her mother shook hands with her, the monkey "immediately became very angry with me, screamed and chattered and threw things at me, being evidently jealous of the attention my mother was paying me."

The jealousy of children, though sometimes exhibited by violent outbreaks, often expresses itself in pouting, sulking, or fits of depression. In adolescence, when jealousy especially in relation to the other sex is so keenly felt, its manifestations are inhibited or diverted still more. Stanley Hall observes, "It is hard for girls to admit that others are more beautiful, witty or cultured than themselves, and rivalry often drives them to extreme and even desperate acts." Sex jealousy is the most common form taken by this emotion in animals and human beings. Nothing arouses the jealousy of a young man or woman so quickly as the danger of being cut out by a rival. Among some Mohammedan peoples the men compel their women to live concealed from the gaze of other men, and permit them to go out only when veiled and attended by an escort. But aside from sex rivalry, jealousy is, in one form or another, exhibited to a certain extent by most people nearly every day of their lives. Professional jealousy among doctors, lawyers, and teachers often colors their opinions of their colleagues to an extent that makes their judgments quite unreliable. Our thoughts about ourselves in relation to others are seldom *entirely* free from this cause of bias.

Most psychologists conclude that jealousy involves both anger and fear, whatever else besides. One fears to lose the object of his affections and at the same time is angry at the individual who may be the occasion of his loss. There may be also anger at the person coveted, as in the occasional instances of young girls who have been murdered by their jealous lovers. But there is, in the jealousy felt by human beings, besides the emotion of fear and anger, an element of wounded pride, or vanity. The jealous man suffers from shame and humiliation in addition to the loss of the object of his affections. There is much truth in the saying of that shrewd old cynic La Rochefoucauld, "There is more self-love than love in jealousy," as is evinced by his other maxim, "Jealousy is always born with love, but does not always die with it."

There are obviously many varieties of jealousy. The jealousy of parrots is little differentiated from anger. The jealousy of Othello is quite different from that of a dog and a monkey. And the sentiment varies from person to person and from time to time. Shand remarks that "at least three emotions, fear, anger, and shame, have left their mark upon it. Thus jealousy seems to reveal no new force of character. It only combines in a peculiar way certain forces that are quite familiar to us."

SHAME

Shame, one of the most powerful of the social emotions, is usually aroused by some sort of disapproval, real or imaginary. It is a negative self-feeling and leads the person to take himself down a peg in his own estimation. It is almost always aroused whenever an individual is caught in an act that incurs the moral condemnation of his associates. If a forbidden act is performed without being found out, the sense of shame aroused may be slight. A student who cheats in an examination without being discovered may suffer very little shame and may even be proud of his cleverness. Neither would he feel much shame if he cheated with the connivance of his fellow students. But if those who knew of his act made him feel that they regarded his conduct with contempt, he would probably feel ashamed of his own action.

It has often been pointed out that shame is aroused by circumstances that have little relation to morality. If one makes himself ridiculous in a social gathering by some *faux pas,* he might suffer an acute sense of shame. The same result would follow an improper exposure of the body. Until recently a Turkish lady would think it disgraceful to permit a view of her face. What arouses a sense of shame is not so much moral dereliction as disapproval. One can hardly escape a feeling of shame even if accused of a shameful act of which he is innocent. He may struggle to suppress this feeling as unreasonable and unjustified, but its depressing effects continue to be felt.

As everyone can testify from his own experience, shame is one of the most powerful factors that influence our conduct. There is almost no incentive that would induce one to perform a very indecent action before a public audience. Even if our life depended on it we could hardly conquer the restraining influence of our sense of shame. And if we should succeed, we would feel shame whenever we recalled our action.

Shame certainly tends to make us moral, though it may not afford the highest moral motive. Leslie Stephen asks, "So far as I am accessible to shame shall I not be inclined to over-estimate the judgment of the class in which I live, to regard decorum as of more importance than real virtue, to make respectability a measure of my conduct ... to obey codes which I disapprove in my heart, such as that which enforces dueling, and to break through moral laws which are generally regretted such as that which condemns bribery; and above all, shall I not feel a much greater fear of being found out than of being guilty?" But while conceding shame is "not identical with conscience and at times might lead to undesirable kinds of conduct," Stephen remarks, that he "should also find it impossible to say that the shame felt by a sinner is not a part of the conscientious feeling or of the intrinsic sanction of morality."

Shame is not always aroused by social disapproval. One may be ashamed of himself for doing something unworthy in his own eyes. As a guest in a friend's house he may have stolen some small article, whose loss never could be discovered, and then despised himself for having stooped to such a contemptible peccadillo. He is a rather sorry specimen of humanity who is not his own mentor. And a sense of shame, that may visit one in the silence of the night, may strongly reinforce the sanction derived from other moral impulses. The biological utility of the sense of shame as a means of social subordination and conformity is very great. It constitutes one of the most deeply ingrained emotions of human nature. Apparently it is felt even by a dog, who may slink away with his tail between his legs, when he is scolded by his master. Such action in a cat can hardly be imagined. But a cat is not a social animal.

BASHFULNESS AND MODESTY

These allied traits are even more completely social than shame. J. Mark Baldwin, who has made one of the best studies of bashfulness, distinguishes three stages in the manifestation of this reaction. Young infants are as devoid of bashfulness as of shame because both these feelings involve the development of self-consciousness and the recognition of one's self as a member of a group. The first appearance of bashfulness is "generally in the first year." The child may try to hide behind its mother's dress with averted gaze, making nervous and awkward movements or even crying. This "primary bashfulness" is regarded by Baldwin as "probably a differentiation of fear." After a period of "toleration of strangers and a liking for persons generally," Baldwin finds a "return of bashfulness in the child's third year or later." "The bashful five-year-old smiles in the midst of his hesitation, draws near to the object of his curiosity, is evidently overwhelmed with the sense of his own presence rather than with that of his new acquaintance, and indulges in actions calculated to keep notice drawn to himself." There is, I think, no single impulse involved in such conduct, but rather a conflict of self-assertion, curiosity and fear, leading to a lot of trials in behavior until a satisfactory adjustment is made to the social situation.

With the onset of adolescence there is a third outcropping of bashfulness and shyness, especially in the presence of members of the other sex of corresponding age. This may be highly modified by social training, and it may be so completely suppressed by the tendency to self-assertion or exhibition as to be no longer felt. But in the bashful swain the mere presence of an attractive member of the other sex, whom he may be visiting, is simply overwhelming. He fidgets nervously, does not know what to do with his hands and feet, blushes on the least provocation, and is too confused in mind to think of anything appropriate to say, and if he ventures upon a remark it is only to be chagrined at its obvious stupidity. He is nevertheless having a wonderful time. Tantalized though he is by being made the sport of two opposing impulses that mysteriously well up within him, he looks forward to repeating his visit.

It is especially in connection with this shyness of adolescence that the curious reaction of blushing is so frequently manifested. Blushing seems to be an exclusively human trait associated with the feelings of shame and bashfulness, and it is more common in girls than in boys and men. Darwin has given an extended and interesting account of it with his usual thoroughness. As the face is suffused with blood the brain is also, and it is probable that this sudden engorgement of the cerebral blood vessels is responsible for the confusion of thought which frequently accompanies the reaction. Darwin was clearly puzzled to explain the origin of blushing and his tentative hypothesis, which involves an appeal to Lamarckian inheritance, is not satisfactory; nor have the subsequent theories of Baldwin and others been much more successful. Biologically, bashfulness and shyness are reactions that tend to suppress individual assertion in ways that do not meet with approval. Bashful people are averse to standing out from the herd in any conspicuous relation. They like to take comfort in the obscurity of likeness to their fellows. Most of us recall vividly our early discomfort in appearing before an audience. Stage fright may completely paralyze all thought and make the victim wish he could sink through the floor. The bashful individual is in the grip of a powerful herd instinct which says to him, "Who are you to put yourself forward? Get back into the ranks where you belong."

Bashfulness and shyness make for conformity. They tend to cause the social suppression of the otherwise bumptious and too independent person and to encourage an attitude of meek submissiveness. This function was probably more important in former ages when more stress was laid upon uniformity of behavior and attitude. If the individual acts in a way that makes himself an object of attention, he has to overcome the tendency to slink back into the uniformity of the herd. The adventure is accompanied by a certain amount of trepidation and confusion of thought. And here, I think, may lie an interpretation of the puzzling phenomenon of blushing. Certainly the blush does not render the individual more efficient, and it would seem to have no particular social utility. But the cerebral and not the cutaneous engorgement of blood vessels, and the accompanying confusion of thought have the effect of inhibiting the actions of the individual and causing him to retreat into the security of herd likeness. In other words, blushing is an incidental accompaniment of a reaction which tends to suppress conspicuous nonconformity. It is nature's device to paralyze egregiousness. She suppresses the offender by covering him with confusion.

PRIDE

Among the sentiments which make man a moral animal, pride occupies a prominent place. It is a form of positive self-feeling correlative with the antithetic feelings of shame and humiliation. Pride can only develop on a basis of self-consciousness whereby an individual recognizes himself as a member of a community of persons whose attitude toward himself is a matter of concern. The proud man, Darwin observes, "exhibits his sense of superiority over others by holding his head and body erect. He is haughty (haut), or high, and makes himself appear as large as possible; so that metaphorically he is said to be swollen or puffed up with pride." The whole attitude "stands in direct antithesis to humility."

As contrasted with shame, pride tends to be associated with efforts at display, when it easily passes into vanity. A purely selfish pride often leads to a supercilious disregard of the general welfare, but as a component of self-respect it is a powerful influence in checking impulses to acts contrary to the ideals that one sets up for himself. It is therefore an important element in the conscience of every upright man. Though repeatedly held up to scorn as contrasted with the virtue of humility, and referred to as "the first peer and president of Hell" (Dryden), and "the never failing vice of fools," pride with all its faults is one of the great mainstays of morality.

SYMPATHY

If I am unexpectedly aroused by hearing a succession of loud screams in an adjoining room, I cannot fail to be profoundly moved. The mere physical shock of the experience may leave me quite unnerved. I am impelled to rush to the spot from which the screams come to render any assistance that the circumstances may require, but my emotions and my actions arise without reflection. They are impulsive like those of an animal moved by the cries of distress uttered by its young.

Such acts have commonly been regarded as prompted by instinctive sympathy. But it is questionable if sympathy *per se* can properly be said to rest upon an instinctive basis. Unlike typical instincts it may be aroused by all sorts of objects and responded to in all sorts of ways. As is implied by its etymology, sympathy involves the ability to share the feelings of another individual. To a certain extent we may feel another's pleasure or another's pain. We are prone to laugh when witnessing the laughter of other people, and we are depressed by seeing expressions of sorrow. This tendency to reflect the moods and the feelings of one's associates is not necessarily conducive to moral behavior, although it is often a great aid to morality. It helps to make people more nearly alike in their feelings and actions, but it may make them alike in doing wrong things.

Sympathy is closely related to imitation and suggestion. Tarde, who lays great stress on imitation as a social factor ("La Société c'est l'imitation"), makes sympathy and suggestion varieties of imitative activity; and Baldwin speaks of sympathy as "imitative emotion par excellence." Obviously the ability to share, or feel with, the feelings of another is conducive to altruistic behavior. If we are callous to suffering, we should not be so strongly impelled to relieve it, but sympathy alone would not make a good Samaritan. Some sensitive persons might be much distressed by the sight of suffering and would simply turn away to avoid the unpleasant sight. Most of us shrink instinctively from witnessing scenes that arouse disagreeable sympathetic feelings. No one would willingly look upon a surgical operation on one dear to him, especially in the days before anesthetics. Those who are disposed to take a cynical view of human nature might contend that we relieve distress from the purely selfish motive of avoiding sympathetic pains. But whatever may be the satisfaction we derive when acting from motives of sympathy, we act in many cases impulsively and without any thought of our own advantage. Surely we are not always sympathetic with malice aforethought. Nature has made us sympathetic that we may be unselfishly helpful to our fellows.

The close association of sympathy with altruistic behavior has given rise to a prevalent confusion in the use of this term. A person is commonly described as sympathetic when he has a kindly attitude toward his fellows. We are said to sympathize with people when we are sorry for their misfortunes. Since we may have sympathetic fear, and sympathetic anger, and even sympathetic hatred, the denotation of the term as commonly used is not sufficiently broad, but the sympathy that goes along with common efforts to escape, or common activities of attack, may be as biologically advantageous as the sympathy that leads us to help a comrade in distress. These varied kinds of sympathy are manifested in the higher animals as well as in man. There are many well authenticated accounts of dogs showing signs of distress over their master's illness or misfortune. In describing the behavior of monkeys toward a sick comrade Romanes remarks, "It was truly affecting to see with what anxiety and tenderness they nursed the little creature. A struggle often ensued among them for priority in those offices of affection; and some would steal one dainty and some another which they would carry to it untasted." Köhler in *The Mentality of Apes* describes as follows the action of one of his chimpanzees, Tercera, toward her little sick companion, Konsul, who in attempting to join a group, "suddenly fell to the ground with a piercing cry of fear. Tercera was sitting some way away chewing. She sprang up, her hair standing on end all over her body with excitement. She reached him in a few strides, walking upright, her face filled with the utmost concern, her lips protruding with sorrow and uttering sounds of distress; she caught hold of him under the arms and did her best to raise him. One could not imagine anything more maternal than this female chimpanzee's behavior."

In these cases sympathy is closely associated with affection, or the tender emotion. People are more apt to sympathize with those they love than with total strangers, and among lower animals sympathy may be exclusively confined to members of their own species. Some writers have considered that sympathy is the fundamental basis of altruistic behavior. A. Sutherland, for instance, in his extensive and valuable treatise on *The Origin and Growth of the Moral Instinct,* contends that sympathy constitutes a sort of primitive morality, and that, "the other constituents of a more complex morality are all derivatives of sympathy." However, he employs sympathy in a way that fails to distinguish it from the tender emotions. Sutherland traces the gradual evolution of sympathy and affection, from their beginning in the domestic group among primitive animals, through savage and barbaric men to modern civilized mankind. His two volumes constitute a mine of most interesting information on both animal and human morals that is not found elsewhere in the literature of the subject and will repay perusal by all who are interested in evolutionary ethics.

AFFECTION OR THE TENDER EMOTION

One of the great merits of Sutherland's treatise, to which we have just referred, is the emphasis placed upon the importance of parental care in the evolution of the moral emotions. In the care of parents for offspring we have, according to Sutherland, the beginnings of love and all altruistic conduct. Love was born in the family, and only later in evolution did it come to extend to other members of the species.

"Like other primary emotions," McDougall observes, "the tender emotion cannot be described; a person who has not felt it could no more be made to understand its quality than a totally color-blind person can be made to understand the experience of color sensation." On its behavioristic side the emotion prompts to fostering and protecting activities of many sorts. "Girded for service, seeking not its own," it affords the motive for self-sacrifice, even at times the sacrifice of life for others. How to understand the entrance of this benign faculty into this world of strife has been the theme of much theorizing. Some have appealed to a miracle outright in the contention that mere nature would be totally incapable of producing such a faculty. The psychologists of the associationist school have attempted to account for it as compounded somehow of sensations of pleasure resulting from our associations with other people. Professor Bain in

The Emotions and the Will says, "In considering the genesis of the Tender Emotion, in any or all its modes, I am inclined to put great stress upon the sensation of animal contact or the pleasure of the embrace. . . . The soft warm touch, if not a first class influence, is at least an approach to that. . . . The sort of thrill from taking a baby in arms is something beyond mere warm touch. . . . In the contact of male and female there is the additional element of the sex instinct." But, as Bain adds, "The strong fact that cannot be explained away is that under tender feeling there is craving for the embrace. Between sexes, there is the deeper appetite, while in mere tender emotion, not sexual, there is nothing but the sense of touch to gratify, unless we assume occult magnetic influences."

The foregoing well illustrates the rather desperate expedient to which a member of the school of Mr. Bain is compelled to resort in the effort to derive emotion from sensation. That so deep and passionate an emotion as maternal love could be compounded out of sensations such as one receives by handling velvet cushions seems absurd enough. Bain clearly puts the cart before the horse in explaining a mother's thrill in handling the soft body of a baby. If the emotion were not there, the soft touch would not cause much of a thrill.

Spencer's attempt to derive maternal affection from the love of the helpless is no more successful, for the reason that the fundamental source of his failure is the same as that of Bain. If nature had not first made women fond of babies, it is doubtful if they would have been so solicitous over young kittens and poodles. As a matter of history, love of offspring is vastly more ancient than love of helpless creatures in general. In the animal world the helpless, if not gobbled up, are generally treated with entire indifference.

There are obviously many varieties of tender emotion.

Romantic love, love of parents, love of friends, and love of offspring, involve different subjective states and very different objective manifestations. There is great variability also in the extent to which the tender emotion is disinterested. It may be very selfish or very unselfish, and it is futile to attempt, as has frequently been done, to analyze all affection into purely selfish considerations. These who have attempted to do this have usually limited their observations to human beings, but when the matter is viewed from the broader standpoint of comparative psychology, the fundamentally altruistic nature of this emotion becomes clearly apparent. The roots of altruistic behavior strike deep down in the animal kingdom. The way in which animals came to care for one another and to minister to one another's needs has a long and rather curious history. We shall endeavor to indicate briefly some of the probable stages of this development in the subsequent chapter on "The Deep Roots of Altruism."

I have discussed briefly a few of the chief character traits of human beings which appear to depend in large part upon inherited endowments and which help to make man a moral animal. There are several other characteristics whose consideration must be omitted for lack of space, since it is not my aim to write a treatise on human nature or social psychology, but rather to illustrate the application of evolutionary principles in interpreting the moral nature of man. From the Darwinian standpoint these traits must be considered as basically good, if we interpret good as that which conduces to the survival and increase of life. Moral evil means conduct inimical to the life of the individual or the group. In other words, evil is maladjusted conduct. It has often been urged that the Darwinian theory is incapable of explaining the origin of disinterested benevolence. Of this more anon. But it would be equally pertinent to urge that it could not explain the origin of pure cussedness. Ruthless egoism is, of course, plentiful enough, and natural selection has no special difficulty in accounting for it, but the existence of pure malevolence would create a real difficulty for the Darwinian.

Darwin's theory should be able to offer a plausible explanation of why man is moved by fear, anger, disgust, shame, love of offspring, and other fundamental drives of his original nature. It would be absurd to appeal to it to explain why people in Spain are mostly Catholics or why Presbyterianism had such a vogue in Scotland. Man's nature is, as we have pointed out, very susceptible to modification through the effects of experience. His native impulses may be largely inhibited or greatly strengthened by habit. With a normal human inheritance most of us could be made very good or very bad, according to the influences affecting our moral character. Basically we are all much alike. Our characters may be compared to organisms having corresponding, or homologous parts in common, but differing in the relative degrees to which these parts are developed. The skull of a man looks quite different from the skull of a gorilla: both have the same bones in much the same relative positions, but some bones are large in the gorilla and small in man and vice versa. So it is with the character traits of Jones and Smith. Combativeness may be strongly developed in Jones, and Smith may be meek as a lamb, whereas Smith may be very sympathetic and Jones rather callous or even brutal. But neither Smith nor Jones is entirely lacking in the qualities possessed by the other. Their differences are matters of emphasis. A part of these differences comes from the collection of genes with which Jones and Smith started life. But to a great extent they result from the effects of environment and training.

If a boy is brought up in one of the crime areas of Chicago, he almost inevitably runs with a gang, and is very apt to be led first into petty stealing and then into graver forms of crime. His emotional nature is warped by dulling his kindly feelings, intensifying his vengeful proclivities, and in other ways that unfit him for normal social life. He may even become a human fiend and revel in incredible cruelties. Human nature does have the capacity for becoming devilish to an extent that almost tempts one to believe in the love of evil for evil's sake. Children often tease and torture others apparently in the sheer delight of inflicting pain. Jesse Pomeroy, the notorious child murderer, cut the throats of little girls just for the fun of seeing the blood run. Some writers have attempted to account for such diabolical conduct as a survival of the activities of fighting and bloodshedding of primitive men. G. Stanley Hall, in his interesting collection of facts concerning juvenile immoralities and crimes, states, "I can conceive no other clue by which to explain the sad facts of certain types of juvenile torturers than the atavistic one." One may also appeal to the satisfaction of exercising power, or the gratification of curiosity, but possibly different explanations are required for different cases. Sadism associated with sex is a curious aberrant type of behavior whose interpretation presents a puzzling problem. The diabolic tortures that many tribes of American Indians inflicted upon their captives have been explained partly as a result of revenge (a very primitive kind of justice), or as a warning to possible enemies of what may happen to them if they engage in war.

Through the exaggeration and suppression of the inherent impulses of human nature, the changes wrought by experience and learning, and the modifications due to accidents and disease, human beings have become diversified in almost endless ways. One great predisposing circumstance that helps us to understand the great **diversity** of human character has been pointed out by William James. "Nature," he says, "implants contrary impulses to act on many classes of things, and leaves it to slight alterations in the conditions of the individual case to decide which impulse shall carry the day. Thus, greediness and suspicion, curiosity and timidity, coyness and desire, bashfulness and vanity, sociability and pugnacity, seem to shoot over into each other as quickly, and to remain in as unstable equilibrium, in the higher birds and mammals as in man. They are all impulses, congenital, blind at first, and productive of motor reactions of a rigidly determinate sort. *Each one of them, then, is an instinct,* as instincts are commonly defined. *But they contradict each other*—experience in each particular opportunity of application usually deciding the issue."

With instincts leading to opposed types of behavior, now the one and now the other would be emphasized by experience and habit. One man might become bold and aggressive and another timid and retiring, or one person might become sympathetic and another brutal, depending upon which of his native reaction types was most frequently or forcibly brought into action. Experience selects from the repertoire of native drives and random activities those types of behavior that are called out in the environment of the developing individual.

A great deal of what we condemn as bad in human conduct is the result of egoistic impulses that lead to acts inimical to the welfare of others. Egoism is, of course, all very well in its place. It is really the first and, on the whole, the most important of all the virtues. Spencer very pertinently observes, "Ethics has to recognize the truth, recognized in unethical thought, that egoism comes before altruism. The acts required for continued self-preservation, including the enjoyments of benefits achieved by such arts, are the first requisites to universal welfare. Unless each duly cares for himself, his care for all others is ended in death, and if each thus dies there remain no others to be cared for."

That nature has equipped man with a generous allotment of egoistic impulses is well exemplified in any nursery. The young child attempts to grab everything he wants, whether another child has it or not, and it is only after much experience that he becomes mindful of the rights and pleasures of others. Many people continue throughout life to disregard the feelings of other individuals, and the supreme selfishness of criminals is a matter of frequent comment. Although the evils resulting from uncontrolled egoism are very great, there are also grave evils caused by misguided altruism. Much mischief is done by unwise efforts to do good. Many a child has been spoiled through the unselfish sacrifices of a well-meaning but unwise mother or grandmother. Most anti-vivisectionists are doubtless actuated by a humanitarian spirit in their endeavors to prohibit animal experimentation, to which humanity owes so great a debt, but the harm they would do, if they had their way, surpasses all power of calculation.

Altruism, like egoism, may be good or bad. It receives much the greater meed of praise because, unlike egoism, it requires all the encouragement that can be given if it is forthcoming to the extent needed for the general weal. After all, human nature is only imperfectly adapted to the needs of social life. In the degree to which our nature is modified to promote social as compared with individual well-being, we are hardly comparable with the hive bees and the termites. Man has passed so quickly from the status of small nomadic groups under the leadership of some old patriarch to all the complexities of modern social life, that one cannot expect his original nature to be very well adjusted to his new conditions of existence. Unlike the bees and the termites, man requires a deal of education and discipline to fit him even passably for his new rôle. That he has been able to achieve even the indifferent success that he has made is, I think, a remarkable fact. It is only within relatively recent times, geologically speaking, that man sprang from his apelike ancestors. With all his great intellectual advances over his progenitors, he is still very much like them emotionally and temperamentally. He still has the same fundamental drives, although they are greatly obscured and modified by early and extensive conditioning.

In his endeavors to know himself, man has obtained some of his most illuminating insights by directing his attention away from his own personality and studying the ways of animals. History shows only too plainly that man has never really understood man. He has acquired all sorts of false and artificial conceptions of human nature and its workings. Let anyone read such books as Lecky's *History of European Morals,* Westermarck's *History of Moral Ideas,* Hobhouse's *Morals in Evolution,* or Sumner's *Folkways,* and note the many ways in which false conceptions of human nature and of man's relations to his world have resulted in all sorts of harmful and cruel conduct, and he will form some faint conception of the tragedies resulting from man's ignorance of himself. Believing the insane to be possessed by devils, he has kept them chained in filthy dungeons and flogged them for their ravings. Believing that all sorts of misfortunes are caused by the use of magical powers, he has killed and tortured thousands of innocent people for witchcraft and sorcery. Believing in a Hell in which people are burned eternally for holding wrong opinions on matters of theology, he has tortured and killed thousands more in the effort to stamp out heresy. For ages he has lived in terror of creatures of his own imagination in the form of demons and other maleficent supernatural beings. Only as science, the true

Messiah, has given man a better understanding of his own nature, have these and many other evils been dispelled.

But many other evils remain which a better understanding of man will doubtless help us to remove. Herbert Spencer made the very wise remark that mind can be understood only by knowing how mind is evolved. The theory of evolution has contributed greatly to the scientific understanding of human nature, and the results have found practical applications in psychology, education, medicine, and other human disciplines. The changing conceptions of man are even beginning to have some effect in politics and economics. But with all the knowledge of man that has thus far been acquired, he is still very much of an enigma, and many of us in these days feel quite uncertain as to what can be expected of him. Those who are concerned with making something better out of man are apt to find that at times he is disappointingly intractable. Certainly he is no angel. In the light of his quadrumanous derivation it is, of course, too much to expect that he would, or could be. But we must also concede that he owes much of his natural goodness to his animal ancestry. With all his faults, it is a fact in which the practical reformers are entitled to take much consolation, that, with the right kind of management, he can be greatly improved. Human welfare, as we have seen, has been greatly enhanced, and many evils were dispelled as man acquired a more rational conception of his own nature. But man has still much to learn about himself before he can make his future secure.

CHAPTER VII

The Deep Roots of Altruism

> Biologists have shown that there are a number of disinterested instincts, and that the preservation of the species depends on the inheritance of such instincts of the offspring.
> —A. F. SHAND, *The Foundations of Character*

MORALISTS HAVE LONG been greatly troubled over the matter of altruism. They have often wondered if man is capable of being really and truly altruistic. Many Christian philosophers, like Luther, would have us believe that everything that is good in man comes by the grace of God, and that intrinsically man is merely a vile worm with no goodness in his own proper nature. On the other hand, many rationalists, with no theological prepossessions worth speaking of, held that man is entirely self-centered in everything he does and thinks. The egoistic hedonists have it that man performs good acts only in the hope of benefits in return or for the self-satisfaction he derives by doing them. In contrast to these rather depressing views of human nature, we have the rosy and romantic pictures which Rousseau and his followers have given us of natural man as a creature essentially pure and good.

It is a fact of common observation, interpret it how we will, that people derive much pleasure from doing good acts. There are countless kindly souls who are never so happy as in relieving distress or in some other kind of well doing for others. And this raises the question, Why did people come to be constituted in this particular way? The common answer given by the adherents of several ethical creeds is that God made people with benevolent impulses that prompt them to do good to others. But this answer was hardly satisfactory to the rationalist seeking for naturalistic explanations. Attempts to give a scientific account of the origin of altruistic sentiments and conduct were made by the associationist school from Hartley to J. S. Mill and Bain. Disinterested affection, they thought, must be derived somehow from the simpler elements of sensation, the original components of ideas. Association was conceived to be the great fundamental principle by which, through a sort of psychological alchemy, the baser elements of sensation could be transmuted into the gold of the higher moral sentiments. From this standpoint all the emotions and sentiments that we experience, however unselfish they may seem to be, are built of simpler psychological components that are primarily egoistic in function.

But, it may be asked, does not the acceptance of the doctrine of evolution compel us to derive the altruism of man from the egoism of his animal ancestors? Can the Darwinian theory, which attributes the evolution of man to the survival of favorable variations in the struggle for existence, explain the origin of a creature who really enjoys being helpful to his fellows? The answer commonly given is a triumphant No! The plausibility of the answer is based on the implied assumption that you cannot derive altruism from egoism if you admit that, in the last analysis, altruism really exists. Let us look at this fundamental assumption a little more closely.

Nothing is apparently more unselfish than maternal love. But if we go far enough down in the animal kingdom, we find creatures that do not show the least trace of it. It must have come about somehow during the evolution of life. From what did it spring? And if maternal love was derived from something different, must we not derive all kinds of altruism from activities that are not altruistic?

My answers to these two questions are: (1) that maternal affection was very slowly evolved, not from egoism, but from other kinds of essentially altruistic behavior, and (2) that the latter go back in some form to the very beginning of life. Properly speaking, altruism does not grow out of egoism; both are exhibited even in the simplest of all known organisms. The activities of all living creatures, as Aristotle long ago pointed out, center about two ends, the maintenance of the individual and the perpetuation of its kind. In all life there are the primal roots of both egoism and altruism. The fission of the simplest organism is an altruistic process in that it has to do with the promotion of more than the individual life. In other words, egoism and altruism are coeval instead of successive developments.

As we pass up the scale of life, both the self-preserving and the race-perpetuating processes become more and more complex. Life had not advanced very far before reproduction became associated with sex. Among primitive multicellular animals sexual reproduction is, as a rule, accomplished by simply discharging eggs and sperm cells into the water and leaving their union to chance. There is no union of the sexes, but simply a union of sex cells. The young, which develop from the fertilized eggs, shift for themselves without the least aid from either of their parents. Reproduction does not involve any behavior on the part of parents beyond the simple vegetative processes of producing and discharging sex cells.

Even among animals quite high in the scale of life, having complex organs of reproduction and more or less elaborate sex behavior subservient to securing the meeting and fusion of eggs and sperm, parents may not pay the slightest attention to their young. Most worms, crustaceans, arachnids, mollusks, and insects are totally indifferent to the fate of their offspring. There is considerable evidence for the view that parental care did not first appear full-blown, but gradually developed out of activities associated with reproduction. Let us see how this transition may have occurred.

Among the insects, for instance, the eggs, as a rule, are not simply laid, but laid in special ways. The female dragonfly deposits her eggs in the water in which the young pass their larval life. The cabbage butterfly fastens her eggs to cabbages or other related plants that supply the food requirements of the larvae. The housefly prefers horse manure, and the blowflies and the fresh flies are careful to lay their eggs on animal flesh, if somewhat putrid so much the better. The solitary bee, *Osmia papaveris,* excavates a hole in the ground, lines it, in accordance with her fastidious taste, with the petals of a poppy, fills it partly full of pollen and honey, and after depositing an egg upon her store of provisions, fills up the hole with dirt, and leaves her egg to its fate. The young larva, which hatches from it and feeds upon the store of food, the mother bee never sees or knows anything about.

Among the solitary wasps the activities associated with egg-laying become still more complex and specialized. Commonly a hole is dug in the ground; then the mother wasp goes in search of her victim. Some species only capture spiders, others grasshoppers, others the larvae of moths, and others choose only beetles of the family Buprestidae and only a few closely related species of them. After pouncing upon her prey, the wasp stings it, commonly near the ganglia of the ventral nerve cord and thus, as Fabre has shown, causing paralysis but not death. Then lugging her prey back to her hole, she drags it in, lays an egg upon it, fills the hole with dirt and flies off in search of another victim. In all this elaborate performance, which varies much in detail with different species, the activities are gone through blindly and instinctively. Of the larva that will emerge from the egg the wasp knows nothing; does not recognize it as any kin of hers and pays not the least attention to the creature whose needs she had previously provided for with so much pains.

Egg-laying, which is a very simple process in the lower invertebrate animals, becomes elaborated in many different and often complex ways in more highly developed forms. Great pains are taken to deposit eggs in the proper situations, in making nests or cocoons to receive them, and in gathering food for the young that will emerge from them. In some cases eggs are cared for in very queer ways: in being plastered over the back of the Surinam toad, in being carried about by the hind legs of the male obstetrical frog; in being received into the vocal sacs of other frogs; and in being carried in the mouth of the males of some kinds of catfish; but in all these cases there is not the least solicitude for the offspring. All these curious procedures involve structural and behavior modifications which have become associated secondarily with the physiological function of egg-laying. This provides for the welfare of offspring, but love for offspring is not yet born.

Among fishes, although most species pay no attention to their eggs after they are extruded, there are a few species, such as the sticklebacks, which lay their eggs in nests and guard them until they hatch. A few species of reptiles are apparently more or less concerned with the protection of their eggs, and among ants and termites eggs are protected and often carried away from unfavorable situations. But the birds treat their eggs with a solicitude that amounts to a passion. One cannot credit the domestic hen with any premonition of the chicks which will appear after her three-weeks' ordeal of incubation. Her devotion to her task results from pure instinct. After the young chicks emerge and begin to peck and chirp, new instincts are elicited until her brood are able to shift for themselves. But her eggs were her first love.

Among the bees there is a most interesting series of transitional forms from the solitary species, like Osmia, which never see their own offspring, through semisocial forms to species, like the hive bee, which are highly specialized in adaptation to social life. In the primitively social bumblebees the queen, which winters in some protected nook, starts a nest in the spring, makes a few cells of wax, provisions them with pollen and honey, and lays one or more eggs in each. More food may be brought to the cells after the young hatch, and thus a transition may be effected between providing for future offspring and feeding the offspring during their larval growth. In this and other tasks the queen comes to be assisted by her first brood of worker females who take over most of the labors of building cells and collecting food. Generations quite separated in the solitary bees are brought together and a certain amount of parental care thus makes its appearance.

There are some species of fish in which the parent, commonly the male, guards not only the eggs, but also the young for a short period until the brood scatters. Care for eggs comes to be extended to what comes out of the eggs. Eggs apparently were objects of concern long before there was any solicitude of parent for offspring. Parental care was doubtless evolved independently along a number of different lines, and the way in which care came to be extended from eggs to offspring may have varied in different cases. In its beginning it is a blind instinctive procedure, with what emotional accompaniment, if any, one can hardly imagine. But once started it constitutes a step of tremendous importance for the further evolution of life.

Most insects, as we have stated, do not show a trace of parental care, exhibiting at best only some of the accessory reproductive activities which in certain forms might have prepared the way for its eventual appearance. Only in the social insects, in which successive generations have been more or less telescoped together, do we find that the young larvae are the recipients of any active ministrations.

Aside from the social insects and the higher vertebrate animals, active parental care is almost unknown. It blossoms out only rarely and more or less sporadically in remotely related groups of animals, occurring in only a few cases amid a vast amount of varied and often elaborate behavior centering about eggs. Prospective young are provided for long before there is the least concern over or even perception of the actual reality.

Parental care has arisen independently a number of times because the basis from which it has developed is very widespread. In several cases it has been only a feeble efflorescence that has never extended beyond a small group. Only in the birds and the mammals has it taken a firm hold and become a universal characteristic of entire classes. Doubtless in these two groups parental care had an independent origin like warm-bloodedness. Both birds and mammals descended from reptiles, but they are both separated by a very wide gap from their reptilian ancestors. The intermediate stages in the evolution of the instinct of incubation, which is almost universal in birds and which is closely associated with the development of warm-bloodedness, are entirely lost; but there remain in present-day birds many stages in the development of instincts for the care of what emerges from the eggs after the labor of incubation. The more primitive running birds make crude nests or none. The young run about actively immediately after hatching, and the parent birds remain with them for only a short time, usually not more than two or three weeks. Little parental care is needed as the young are soon well able to take care of themselves. Passing to the higher songbirds, and omitting intermediate stages in the development of parental care, we find a very different family life. Commonly there are well constructed nests often lined with down or other soft material; few eggs are laid and the young, which are hatched in a helpless condition, are brooded, fed, and protected by their devoted parents, who spend a large part of their time in ministering to their needs. Without continued parental care the young would quickly perish. There is also a lengthening of the period in which the young birds are cared for by their parents. One often sees a nearly full-grown robin, perfectly able to forage for itself, being supplied with food by its indulgent parents.

Among the mammals parental care had a somewhat similar evolution. The possession of mammary glands, the fundamental structural feature that gives the class its name, implies a close association between mother and offspring and the development of fostering instincts on the part of the one and at least the sucking instinct on the part of the other. The duckbill, which shows many reptilian features in its structure as well as its habit of laying eggs, keeps its young in close contact with its body and nourishes them from its very primitive mammary glands. Parental care in the more primitive mammals seems like an almost mechanized procedure as compared with the demonstrations of maternal affection by dogs and monkeys. Describing a Rhesus monkey which had borne a stillborn baby, Yerkes remarks, "Repeated attempts were made to remove the dead baby but they were futile because Gertie held it in her hands or sat close beside it ready to seize it at the slightest disturbance.... During the second week the body of the corpse was so far decomposed that ... it rapidly wore away. By the third week there remained only the shriveled skin covering a few fragments of bone." Finally, "there existed only a strip of dry skin about four inches long." When Yerkes picked this up, "she made a sharp outcry and sprang to the side of the cage nearest me." On his returning the skin, "she immediately seized it and rushed to the top of the cage."

This pathetic manifestation of maternal attachment to a fragment of her dead offspring, which is exhibited also, according to Zuckermann, by the mother baboon, we are naturally prone to stigmatize as very stupid behavior, although a similar reluctance to keep from parting with their dead is sometimes exhibited by human beings. But if the poor monkey derives an emotional satisfaction in fondling a fragment of her dead baby, why should we call her stupid in obeying her impulse? In the strength of their attachment to their young, and in their demonstrations of affection in many different ways, the apes show a decided approach toward human behavior. Unlike most of the lower mammals, the family ties are not broken until the young attain adolescence. Among gorillas, according to Hartmann, the family group usually consists of an old male, his consort, and a number of offspring of different ages; and Wallace describes similar groups among the orangs. Among the anthropoid apes in general there is a prolongation of infancy, the evolutionary importance of which has been emphasized by John Fiske. In a long period of infancy under the protection of parents, there is opportunity for gaining much experience, through play and other activities, that fits the offspring for the more serious struggles of later life. During this period there is, according to several observers of ape life, a certain amount of discipline administered by parents which helps to maintain the traditional mores of the group.

It is in the family relation that we meet with the earliest

manifestations of true altruistic behavior. Animals in general do not care a fig about other creatures outside of their own domestic circle. A hawk, a rat, or a tiger, all manifest concern for their own offspring, but they could look upon the most cruel tortures of all other creatures and be entirely unmoved. Only in the social animals does altruistic conduct extend beyond the family circle and in these, except in certain cases of adopted "guests," it usually does not spread beyond the limits of the social group, or at least the species.

There are various kinds of associations of animals and they probably have arisen in different ways, but most well-developed social groups have probably been derived from the expansion of the family. In the social bees and wasps this has clearly been their mode of origin, for most such societies represent the descendants of a single queen who founded the colony. The same statement applies to many species of ants, and among the termites a new nest is made by a pair, male and female, who produce a numerous progeny which may include other reproducers along with the castes of workers and soldiers. In the more highly developed societies of insects the instincts and structures of the members are often highly specialized in adaptation to communal life. The worker hive bee lives a strenuous life of unselfish toil for the common weal. If she stings an enemy and thereby loses her life, the group profits by her pugnacity, even if one of its members is lost. In several species of ants and termites there is a special warrior caste with large heads and strong jaws. When these soldiers rush forth and bury their jaws in the flesh of their enemies, they often allow their body to be pulled away from their head before they relinquish their hold. From the standpoint of individual welfare no conduct could be more foolish. This bulldog tenacity is but a part of the life of self-sacrifice which is so conspicuous a trait of all the higher social insects.

It is a curious fact that the fighting instinct of these

insects is almost entirely a group pugnacity. An individual ant, bee, wasp, or termite isolated from its group rarely resents any interference with its activities. The thing that arouses the ire of these creatures is any molestation of their nest. Stir up an ant hill, a hornets' nest, or a hive of bees, and the hostile response will be prompt and decided. There is nothing selfish about their pugnacity; it is an altruistic offering for the general weal. Most insects are as peaceful as lambs, even more so. Those which are fitted with biting or piercing mouth parts seldom employ these organs, except in securing food, or more rarely as a defense against being seized; they are almost never aggressively pugnacious. In animal societies pugnacity and mutual aid are complementary traits. Social insects commonly do not quarrel over which individual will have a particle of food or other object of desire. Aside from the curious, deadly rivalry of queen bees, their animosity, unlike that of human beings, is almost exclusively reserved for enemies of the group. Even in the presocial stage, pugnacity is commonly directed toward the defense of mates and more especially the young. When the domestic group develops into the society the pugnacious instincts become intensified and are employed for the defense of the wider circle of associates. It is a noteworthy fact that organized societies in insects have sprung up only in species that are provided with organs that enable them to bite or sting or both. Without some fighting equipment to start with, a defensive society, as most animal societies are, could not make a beginning.

As Darwin pointed out, the evolution of altruistic social instincts was doubtless brought about by natural selection in which the group, rather than the individual, constitutes the unit in the struggle for existence. By this means, instincts injurious to the individual may be evolved if they conduce to group survival. Even in the family group qualities may be preserved that are not conducive to individual welfare. The labors of nest-building, incubation, feeding the young, and protecting them in face of danger bring no advantage to the individual as such. Reproduction is a function that often entails great sacrifices and dangers. In the parasitic threadworm, *Rhabditis nigrovenosa,* the young, which are hatched within the body of the mother, proceed to devour her internal organs, after which the young matricides eat their way out. Here the individual is regularly sacrificed that the race may be reproduced. What natural selection is interested in preserving, if I may be permitted this figurative expression, is not so much the individual as the stream of life, or what Galton called the stirp.

Individuals are mere pawns in the game to be sacrificed as the game or race survival demands. "So careful of the type she seems, so careless of the single life," Nature has first evolved altruistic behavior as an accessory to successful reproduction. But antecedent to the activities that we ordinarily designate as behavior, in the sense in which this term is employed in comparative psychology, there are the physiological processes of producing, storing, and discharging germ cells, and in viviparous animals, carrying and nourishing the young. These processes, though mainly unconscious, are nevertheless altruistic in that they conduce to maintaining life in another individual. Altruism has emerged, starting with the fission of the simplest organism; then it is expressed in more complex ways in the reproductive activities of higher forms, and later manifested in overt behavior with its accompanying sensory and emotional experiences. Naturally its first manifestation occurs in the family. As the family expands into the larger social group, unselfish aid is given to other individuals of the community, but true to its method of origin, its benefits are typically confined to the group. Universal benevolence is not a characteristic of the animal world.

Among none of the higher vertebrates are the individuals so completely subordinated to a social order, as they are in the organized societies of insects. There are no castes and no permanent divisions of functions. Among the herds of herbivorous animals the function of protection devolves mainly upon the older males. In both birds and mammals there may be sentinels whose function is to warn the group of the approach of danger. Although flocks and herds do not usually arise through the expansion of the family, they are largely the result of instincts which had been evolved for their utility in domestic relationships. The various calls that serve to unify the social group or to apprise members of danger doubtless had their basis in the calls of parents to their young. The defense of a member of a group that may be attacked, often involving responses to cries of distress, has its foundation ready at hand with only slight modifications in the instincts of parents to defend their young. All that is needed to account for most of the social instincts of the higher vertebrates is an extension of domestic behavior to later stages of life and its application to a wider group. The foundations of social behavior are thus broadly laid in the family circle.

Passing over the social behavior of the birds and lower mammals, it may be instructive to consider briefly some of the social reactions of man's nearest relatives, the anthropoid apes. "The group connection of chimpanzees," says Köhler, "is a very real force. . . . This can be clearly seen in any attempt to take one animal out of a group which is used to hanging together. . . . The first and greatest desire of the separated creature is to get back to his group. Very small animals are naturally extremely frightened, and show their fear to such a degree that one simply has not the heart to keep them apart any longer. Bigger animals, who do not show signs of actual fear, cry and scream and rage against the walls of their stockade, and if they see anything like a way back, they will risk their very lives to get back to the group. Even after they are quite exhausted from their outbursts of despair, they will crouch, whimpering, in a corner, until they have recovered sufficient strength to renew their raging." The animals within the group are less disturbed over the isolation of one of their members, but "one cannot say that they listen to his wailings without any sympathy. It often happens, that if it is only possible for them to get near the prisoner's cage, one or other of the animals will rush to it and put his arms around him through the bars. But he has to howl and cry for this affection to be shown him."

Man's altruism represents the last stage of a long eventful history. From the fission of the simplest conceivable form of life to the unselfish devotion of a Florence Nightingale or a John Howard, life processes subservient to the welfare of others have gradually evolved through hundreds of millions of years. After all, altruism is just a part of life, and it is as old as life itself. Though it may lead to self-sacrifice, it is always loyal to the group. True to its method of origin, individual altruism is primarily group egoism. Were it not for this fact, it never could have come into existence at all. This also explains many peculiarities of the altruistic behavior of human beings, as will be pointed out in the following chapter dealing with the evolution of moral conduct from savage to civilized mankind.

CHAPTER VIII

The Moral Savage

> When we study the moral rules laid down by the customs of savage peoples we find that they, in a very large measure, resemble the rules of civilized nations.
> —L. T. Hobhouse, *Morals in Evolution*

HAVING BRIEFLY TRACED the evolution of altruism from its foreshadowings in the reproductive activities of primitive animals, and sketched its developments in the domestic group and its gradual spread, with the evolution of societies, to other individuals outside the family, it may be instructive to follow some steps of its further course during man's cultural evolution. Obviously this topic can here be treated only in the barest outline. The readers who desire to acquaint themselves with further details may be referred to the works of Spencer, Sutherland, Hobhouse, Sumner and, above all, Westermarck, whose *Origin and Development of the Moral Ideas* is a mine of instructive information on the natural history of human morals.

During the past century the labors of anthropologists have thrown a flood of light upon the moral practices of the various tribes and races of men. The sympathetic and unbiased study of primitive peoples has dispelled many erroneous ideas and has given us quite different conceptions of savage life from those previously held. Many observers have been greatly shocked by encountering customs which are commonly condemned by civilized peoples. The savage has been held up as cruel, treacherous, lustful, and given over to many practices of the most revolting description. Pious missionaries have dilated upon the immorality of the savage as a horrible example of the effects of ignorance of the revealed moral code. The benighted heathen without the law, being guided only by the impulses of their corrupted human nature, could not be expected to do otherwise than indulge in all sorts of wickedness. Tylor has remarked that, "for the most part the religious world is so occupied in hating and despising the beliefs of the heathen, whose vast regions of the globe are painted black on the missionary maps, that they have little time left to understand them." Others, whose relations with primitive people have been mainly hostile, have had their judgments hopelessly warped thereby, as is illustrated by the once common remark that the only good Indian is a dead Indian. A real understanding of savage life and thought is not easily gained. Even trained observers, who have lived with primitive peoples and have learned their language, often have difficulty in obtaining a true conception of the savage's feelings and ideas. This is especially true of religious beliefs concerning which there are many instances of diametrically opposed assertions made by different observers regarding the same people.

On the whole the information gained by critical and sympathetic studies of primitive morality has placed the savage in a more favorable light. Public opinion is a strong force in controlling his conduct. "Primitive man," says R. H. Lowie, "wants, above all, to shine before his fellows, he craves praise and abhors the loss of 'face.' .... A primitive man sacrifices half his property lest he be dubbed a miser; he yields his wife if jealousy is against the code; he risks life itself if that is the way to gain the honor of a public eulogy." All peoples of the earth have moral codes. And among all codes there is a broad basis of agreement as to the acts which are forbidden or approved. "In every savage community," says Westermarck, "homicide is prohibited by custom and so is theft." Bravery, generosity, hospitality, and kindliness are extolled, and cowardice, deceit, and disloyalty are condemned. At the same time there is much variation in the details of their practices and prohibitions. We are naturally shocked by such customs as infanticide, eating human flesh, the killing of old men and women, and the torture of enemies. But it would be absurd to attribute such acts to the natural depravity of those who take part in them. The true student of the natural history of morals approaches the study of such customs in a purely objective spirit, with the aim of ascertaining the causes that have led to their adoption. And more or less plausible explanations of their origin may often be given by a study of the conditions of life under which the tribe lives. The widespread custom of infanticide, for instance, is a very natural attempt to obviate the evils of an undue increase of numbers. Even in civilized countries, such as China and ancient Greece and Rome, the custom was extensively practiced. Many peoples destroy sickly and deformed infants, children born out of wedlock, and in some cases twins, under the assumption that at least one of them must have been illegitimate. While superstitious notions of many kinds have led to infanticide, its main cause is economic. Its prevalence does not imply any lack of parental affection, because peoples who practice it often show an extravagant fondness for their children, who have been suffered to live beyond perilous days of infancy. Where infanticide is practiced the moral sentiments regarding it have usually been molded by the exigencies of life.

A similar statement probably applies in part to the killing of the old and infirm. This practice is more common in nomadic tribes than in those of fixed abode. Morgan says of the American Indians that, "Among the roving tribes of the wilderness the old and the helpless were frequently abandoned and, in some cases, hurried out of existence as an act of greater kindness than desertion," while among the Iroquois who, "resided in permanent villages the practice was not followed." When Kolben expostulated with the Hottentots on the cruelty of putting old people to death, he was met with the reply, "Is it not a cruelty to suffer either man or woman to languish any considerable time under a heavy, motionless old age? Can you see a parent or a relative shaking and freezing under a cold, dreary, heavy, useless old age and not think of putting an end to their misery?" Among savages old age with its infirmities is often a very miserable period of life, and it has become a tradition in many tribes for the aged to ask to be relieved from the burdens of living. In Fiji, according to Dr. Seeman, "The son will kiss and weep over his aged father as he prepares him for the grave, and will exchange loving farewells with him as he heaps the earth lightly over him." Still more shocking to our own sensibilities is the custom of eating the bodies of aged relatives who have been put to death. In this case the custom seems to be in the nature of a religious ceremony rather than the satisfaction of hunger. On the whole the killing of parents, which is regarded by most people as the most heinous of crimes, is largely motivated by compassion. In some cases, however, more utilitarian considerations have probably been operative also.

Less creditable to primitive peoples is the fairly common practice of leaving the sick and the infirm to die of exposure or from starvation. Some tribes kill their sick, if they are thought to be dangerously ill, or bury them before they are dead. According to Westermarck, "The most common motive for abandoning or destroying sick people seems to be the fear of infection or of demoniacal possession, which is regarded as the cause of various diseases." Dorman states that among the North American Indians "the custom of abandoning the infirm or sick arose from a superstitious fear of the evil spirits which were supposed to have taken possession of them."

Practices which are inhuman in our eyes have given savages quite generally a reputation for callousness and cruelty. Even Sir John Lubbock describes the savage as "almost entirely wanting in moral feeling." Whether the savage is, on the whole, more cruel than civilized man may well be doubted. The American Indians have probably been exceeded by no other savage tribes for the fiendish tortures they inflicted upon their enemies taken in battle. Captives were often turned over to the women who took a special delight in inflicting the most prolonged and painful tortures that ingenuity could devise. But even these diabolical tortures are fully equalled by those of the thumbscrew, the boot, the rack, and the burnings at the stake, which were visited upon tens of thousands of victims during the Inquisition and which continued to be visited upon criminals down to recent times. In the treatment of his enemies even highly civilized man easily reverts to savagery.

One of the most conspicuous features of the moral practices of primitive peoples is that there is one code of conduct toward the members of the group and a very different one toward the outsider. "Morality," says Hobhouse, "is in its origin group morality." In this respect it shows its filiation with the morality of animals. Hostility to strange creatures is a deeply ingrained trait of animal life. A dog is naturally sociable and enjoys the companionship of others of his kind, but a strange dog is regarded with suspicion. Acquaintance is made cautiously after many preliminary sniffs and sometimes growls at undue familiarities. Neither dog is assured as to whether fighting or friendship will result from the encounter, and each must be prepared for eventualities. Only after each dog has learned what to expect in the responses of the other is there a development of confidence and stable friendship.

A very instructive instance of reaction to strangers on the part of chimpanzees is narrated by Köhler. A new female chimpanzee, which was brought into the collection and kept for a time in a separate apartment, became an object of the greatest interest, and the other chimpanzees would endeavor to poke at her with sticks, and on one occasion a stone was thrown against her cage. "When the new-comer, after some weeks, was allowed into the large animals' ground in the presence of the older animals, they stood for a second in stony silence. But hardly had they followed her few uncertain steps with staring eyes, when Rana, a foolish but otherwise harmless animal, uttered their cry of indignant fury, which was at once taken up by all the others in frenzied excitement. The next moment the new-comer had disappeared under a raging crowd of assailants, who dug their teeth into her skin and who were only kept off by our most determined interference while we remained. Even after several days the eldest and the most dangerous of the creatures tried over and over again to steal up to the stranger while we were present and ill-treated her cruelly, when we did not notice in time. She was a poor weak creature, who at no time showed the slightest wish for a fight, and there was really nothing to arouse their anger except that she was a stranger." After a time one of the apes gradually made friends with her and defended her against the attacks of the others. Then others became friendly until most of the group were finally won over.

This widespread hostility to the stranger is, as we have already pointed out, a biologically useful and sensible type of response. Fear reactions and fighting are closely associated and have a common end. When a strange creature is effectually disposed of, or escaped from, there is a feeling of greater security. Exhibition of fear and hostility in the presence of strangers is, of course, common in human beings. Sometimes the reception of the new boy at school is more or less analogous to the experience of the young chimpanzee described. The shyness of children in the presence of new acquaintances is doubtless an expression of the same fundamental type of reaction. All of us react toward strangers with a measure of reserve. Being notoriously clannish, like the chimpanzees, we usually feel less confident of people of other races and nationalities than of people of our own kind. It is to be expected, therefore, that this clannishness, which is exhibited by man and animal in ways which are sometimes so curiously similar, should be more clearly manifested in primitive peoples than in those familiar with a wider range of human relationships. Primitive morality is concerned primarily with the welfare of the clan or tribe and incidentally thereto with the destruction of enemies. Dual moral codes, one for the insider and one for the outsider, are therefore the rule among primitive peoples, and to a considerable degree also among advanced nations. Let us consider a few illustrations of this fact.

The Dyaks of Borneo, to whom we have previously referred, have long been notorious as a fierce and cruel people of headhunters. Brooke in describing their life remarks, "Day after day, month after month, it is the same story, a life of watchfulness, flight and fight." In their frequent and often unprovoked forays against neighboring tribes, even women and children are brutally murdered, and the repute of a man with his tribe is measured by the number of heads that he has to his credit. In their communal life, however, these Dyaks, and especially the more warlike ones, are described as "sociable and kindly to one another," loyal and trustworthy. A. R. Wallace states, "They are truthful and honest to a remarkable degree. Crimes of violence among themselves are unknown. In twelve years under Sir James Brooke's rule there had been but one murder within a Dyak tribe." Bock, who has described in detail the brutalities of their wars, says that as regards morality he is "bound to assign to the Dyaks a high place in the scale of civilization," and Ida Pfeiffer found them "honest, good and reserved . . . much more so than any other nation I know."

Many pages could be filled with illustrations of the kindness, honesty, loyalty, and other virtues among savages who are cruel and unreliable to a degree in their dealings with outsiders. Probably no moral trait is subject to such remarkable variations in different peoples of the earth as veracity. The Veddahs of Ceylon can hardly understand that it is possible for anyone wilfully to say anything that is not true, and Nevill states, "I never knew a Veddah to tell a lie." According to Elliot, "a Kurubar always speaks the truth," and Morgan says, "On all occasions, and at whatever peril, the Iroquois spoke the truth without fear and without hesitation," and other tribes of American Indians had an equally good reputation for veracity. On the other hand the Chipewyans, according to Westermarck, "carry lying to such an extent that they can scarcely be said to esteem truth as a virtue." Gason says of the Dieri of South Australia, "They imbibe treachery in infancy and practice it until death, and have no sense of wrong in it." The Greenlanders who, according to Dielanger, are honest among themselves, told frightful lies in their dealings with Danish traders, and the Tuareg, according to Westermarck, "whilst scrupulously faithful to a promise given to one of their own people, do not regard as binding a promise given to a Christian."

The Masai, says the same author, "hold any kind of deceit to be allowable in their relations with persons of another race."

There are probably no better illustrations of dual codes of ethics than those found in the Old Testament. Truthfulness, chastity, obedience, and justice were enjoined upon the chosen people in their dealings with one another, but those outside the fold were given far less consideration. In Deuteronomy the faithful are given the command, "Ye shall not eat of anything that dieth of itself: thou shalt give it unto the stranger that is in thy gates, that he may eat it; of thou mayest sell it unto an alien." And in waging war the Children of Israel acted with a barbarity unusual even among savages. In approaching a city they were instructed first to proclaim peace unto it. If the city did not abjectly surrender, in which case all the inhabitants were to become tributaries, then it should be besieged, "And when the Lord thy God hath delivered it into thine hands, thou shalt smite every male thereof with the edge of the sword: But the women, and the little ones, and the cattle, and all that is in the city, even all the spoil thereof, shalt thou take unto thyself."

After their victorious war against the Midianites the Children of Israel were commanded by Moses to "kill every male among the little ones, and kill every woman that hath known man by lying with him. But all the women children, that have not known a man by lying with him, keep alive for yourselves." Such shocking atrocities, which seem to have been quite characteristic of the Children of Israel in their more warlike days, exhibit only an extreme form of the widespread tendency to restrict the sphere of sympathy and good will to the members of a single group. In the later writings of the Old Testament we find transitional changes of attitude leading to a conception of a God of all the nations of the earth instead of a tribal deity, and of an era of peace and good will when "nation shall not lift up sword against nation, neither shall they learn war any more."

But throughout the history of the world the complementary qualities of mutual aid and prowess in fighting have been extolled by all peoples. Except for a few tribes living in isolated regions or under unusual conditions, war commonly recurs after variable intervals of time. In no people has war been a chronic condition as it was conceived to be by Hobbes in man's primitive state of nature. Many nations have enjoyed long periods of peace, but the possibility of war has always been sufficiently menacing to prevent an ethics based exclusively on amity from being practiced, instead of merely professed, by any considerable portion of mankind.

Although progress toward mitigating the great evils of war has been discouragingly slow, other expressions of man's pugnacious impulses have been subjected to a high degree of control. In the rudest forms of society the redress of injuries fell to the lot of the individual concerned or his immediate kin. Acts prompted by revenge afford a sort of rough and ready justice which, crude though it be, is better than none. Retaliation is the natural preventive of aggression. In the animal world it is the only way of punishing the infliction of an injury. And it is not surprising that this primitive animal method of squaring accounts should be carried over into the early stages of human culture.

Among the Australian tribes, according to Sir George Grey, "The holiest duty a native is called on to perform is that of avenging the death of his nearest relation, for it is his peculiar duty to do so, and until he has fulfilled this task he is constantly taunted by the old women; his wives, if he be married, would quit him; if he is unmarried not a single young woman would speak to him, his mother would constantly cry and lament she should ever have given birth to so degenerate a son." Nelson states that among the Eskimos of Bering Strait the duty of avenging a murder falls upon the nearest relative; if this is a very young son he must take revenge as soon as he attains puberty. Similar customs of blood revenge were common among North American Indians, and indeed among many peoples of the earth in certain stages of culture. It still persists in Albania and Corsica, and blood feuds have not been long extinct in some of our own states.

Most savages distinguish sharply between killing a member of the tribe and killing an outsider, even in time of peace. Among the Kafirs killing strangers "could hardly be considered a crime" (Robertson). In Savage Island the killing of another tribesman was considered "a virtue rather than a crime," for he was regarded as a potential enemy. J. R. B. Love, in investigating the murder of two strangers who had become stranded on the coast of Western Australia, asked the men implicated, "Was there not one of you who could take pity on these two men?" "No," they said, "They could not talk to us so we had to kill them." Westermarck states, "The Australian Black nurtures an intense hatred of every male of his own race who is a stranger to him and would never neglect to assassinate such a person at the earliest moment that he could do so without risk to himself. In Melanesia also, a stranger as such was generally, throughout the islands, an enemy to be killed."

But along with this widespread hostility to members of alien groups, there have developed customs of recognizing intertribal rights. Although neighboring tribes may remain friendly for a long period, the responsibility for avenging the death of a person belonging to another tribe commonly devolves entirely upon the members of the injured tribe. Such murders are commonly causes of wars and feuds. The tribe is injured in the person of its member as the family unit is injured in intratribal homicides, and if adequate compensation is not given, the tribe of the offender is often attacked.

In more advanced stages of culture, punishment for crime comes to be meted out by the group in the person of its chief or other judicial body instead of the relatives of the injured party. Primitive and barbaric peoples feel very strongly that justice consists in a strict equality of injury and atonement. According to Thurn, among the Guiana Indians "The smallest injury by one Indian to another, even if unintentional, must be atoned for by suffering a similar injury." The classical expression of this attitude is, of course, the *lex talionis:* "Thou shalt give life for life, eye for eye, tooth for tooth, hand for hand, foot for foot." An application of this general principle, involving a third party (apparently not consulted), is found in the custom that a man guilty of adultery has to yield his wife to the injured husband (Waitz).

The notion of justice as getting even somehow with the offender is deeply ingrained even in our modern thought. One often sees it exhibited in the intercourse of children. It is commonly revealed in the more or less childlike remarks on punishment expressed by adults. The feeling of vindictiveness, such as arises in most of us upon reading an account of a shocking crime, may be productive of much injustice, but it may be questioned if without it we should concern ourselves sufficiently to see that justice is done. Doubtless this spirit has prompted the passage of many unjust laws and caused many poor devils to be hanged for petty thefts. But we should not forget that it has played, on the whole, a useful rôle in the long and painful evolution of man's moral behavior.

When we survey the course of man's moral development as he has passed from the early clan stage to more highly civilized societies, there are two outstanding features of the process which cannot fail to impress us. These are: (1) the gradual liberation of the mind from the iron grip of custom and tradition, and (2) the broadening of the range of human sympathy that comes with the development of larger social groups and the increase of human knowledge. Men of the rudest culture live in relatively small and mainly independent groups. Sutherland has estimated that the social units in the lowest groups, such as the Bushmen, Negritos, and Veddahs, range from 12 to about 100. The average unit in his group of "middle savages," which includes the Australian blacks, Hottentots, Fuegians, and Tasmanians, is about 100, whereas in the "upper savages," which include most of the North American Indians, it averages about 360. The various grades of barbarians form societies ranging roughly according to their scale of cultural development from a few thousand to nearly a half-million.

This increase in the size of social units is doubtless in part the cause and in part the effect of advancing culture. Men of the hunting stage with their scattered numbers, crude arts, lack of written language, and primitive and often temporary dwellings, cannot be expected to administer a stable and effective government over a large number of human beings. Such groups tend to disappear before the pressure of pastoral and agricultural peoples. People living by the cultivation of the soil and the prosecution of industry may grow more rapidly in numbers, and although through long periods of history they have been harassed and sometimes conquered by raiding hordes of pastoral nomads, they have now little to fear from their former nomadic rivals. Nationmaking, to use W. Bagehot's phrase, has gone hand in hand with the development of arts, science, and literature that has gradually emancipated men's minds from the thralldom of rigid custom and the superstitions with which customs are so frequently associated. As people are brought more frequently into contact with members of other groups besides their own, either directly or through literature, their narrow clan morality broadens to include all sorts and conditions of men. This extension of sympathy and understanding, and the growing recognition of moral obligations that know no distinctions of nation or race, has led to the hope that even the great evil of war may eventually come to an end as a result of a continuation of the same trend of development. Whether or not this is just a rosy dream I shall discuss briefly in a later chapter, but without venturing to make any confident predictions.

CHAPTER IX

Religion the Handmaid of Morals

>Almost every chapter of this work has borne witness to the enormous influence which the belief in supernatural forces or beings or in a future life has exercised upon the moral ideas of mankind, and has at the same time shown how exceedingly varied this influence has been.
>
>—E. WESTERMARCK, *The Origin and Development of Moral Ideas*

RELIGION AND MORALITY have been intimately associated since the earliest stages of human culture. Man is a religious as well as social animal, and there is much reason to believe it is because he is a social animal that he is religious. After a good deal of controversy it is now pretty well established that there is no tribe of men that does not entertain some form of religious belief. Religion has a powerful hold upon the minds of primitive peoples, and influences their conduct even in the minutiae of everyday life. One cannot, therefore, rightly interpret many features of the behavior of primitive man without a knowledge of his religious beliefs.

One great underlying basis of primitive religion, to say nothing of its more advanced forms, is the doctrine of animism. "Animism," says Tylor, who was the first to use the word as applied to spiritual beings, "is the groundwork of the philosophy of Religion, from that of savages up to that of civilized man." The belief in spirits is almost universal among savage and barbarous peoples. It is closely associated with the nearly universal belief that the human body is animated (note the word) by an indwelling soul. The soul is the principle of life, and when it departs the body dies. Among different peoples the soul is variously identified with the shadow, the image, and especially the breath. To the savage the doctrine of the soul makes a variety of phenomena intelligible that otherwise would be quite mysterious. Why am I able to move my limbs and make my body obey my will? Why does the body die when the breath leaves it? Why do I see a reflection of myself upon looking into a quiet pool? Is it not my soul? And why does my shadow go around with me and imitate all my movements? The Wanika "are afraid of their own shadows; possibly thinking, as other negroes do, that their shadows watch all their actions and bear witness against them" (Spencer). In situations favorable to the production of echoes one hears a voice repeating his every word. Clearly someone is mocking him, but no one can be seen. It must therefore be an invisible spirit. Knowing nothing of the reflection of sound waves, and hearing sound from an intelligent source, the savage draws the reasonable conclusion in the light of his general ideology. Further evidence of the existence of souls is afforded by dreams, which savages often regard as actual occurrences. While one sleeps the soul may leave the body and travel to other places. The New Zealanders held "that during sleep the mind left the body, and that dreams are the objects seen during its wanderings." Or again, in dreams or trances one may be visited by spirits and receive from them valuable knowledge or power. For the savage the belief in spirits gives a reasonable and unified interpretation of these and various other phenomena. Altogether it is a very fine theory.

All about him the savage observes strange unaccountable phenomena. Lightning flashes from the clouds, terrific peals of thunder rend the sky, the sun may be darkened in midday by an eclipse, violent storms may sweep over the land, plants spring up mysteriously out of the ground, and young animals and human beings come as mysteriously from the bodies of their mothers. The savage peoples the world with numerous invisible beings whose activities cause unaccountable happenings on every hand. He draws no sharp line between the natural and the supernatural. Ordinary occurrences he takes as a matter of course, but the unusual and the striking phenomena he interprets as due to some invisible spiritual agency. Natural law is a concept he has not attained.

By postulating the existence of unseen spirits the savage makes his world more intelligible. We may call his beliefs superstitions, but they are in a sense scientific hypotheses, whether or not they originated in a conscious and deliberate effort to explain observed phenomena. If there are spirits actuated by various motives both good and evil, one can explain why the hunt is often unsuccessful, why people sicken and sometimes get better after the medicine man has performed his peculiar rites, why tempests arise, why monstrosities are sometimes born, and why there are thousands of other occurrences of an unusual kind. The theory of animism is therefore eminently satisfactory to the primitive mind. As Spencer remarks, "Primitive ideas are natural, and, under the conditions in which they occur, rational. . . . We marvel at their strangeness, and attribute perversity to those who hold them. This error we must replace by the truth that the laws of thought are everywhere the same; and that, given the data as known to him, the primitive man's inference is the reasonable inference." Although the inferences drawn cannot be said to be the most reasonable ones, primitive peoples, as Dr. Paul Radin has shown, do a lot of hard thinking over their philosophical problems.

If one accepts the animistic theory of primitive man and the beliefs in magic with which it is commonly associated, the various usages that constitute primitive religious practice have a fairly rational basis. "In early religion," says Westermarck, "the most common motive is undoubtedly a desire to avert evils; and we have reason to believe that such a desire was the first source of religious worship. Despite recent assertions to the contrary, the old saying holds true that religion was born of fear. Those who maintain that the savage is little susceptible to this emotion and that he for the most part takes his gods joyously, show ignorance of facts. One of his characteristics is great nervous susceptibility, and he lives in constant apprehension of danger from supernatural powers. . . . From all quarters of the civilized world we hear that terror or fear is the predominant element in the religious sentiment, that savages are more inclined to ascribe evil than good to the influence of supernatural agents, that their sacrifices and other acts of worship more frequently have in view to avert misfortunes than to procure positive benefits or that, even though benevolent deities are believed in, much more attention is paid to malignant ones."

The savage lives in a world peopled with all sorts of beings that he cannot see and about whose attitudes toward himself he is very uncertain. The natural reaction to the unknown is that of fear, especially when the unknown agencies are able to cause all sorts of dire calamities. The wise thing to do, therefore, is to propitiate them. Prayers, gifts, sacrifices, cajolery, threats, and the exercises of magical powers of compulsion, are all resorted to under different circumstances in order to enjoy a satisfactory *modus vivendi* with these unseen powers. Supernatural beings not only affect man, but man, through the exercise of magical powers, which he secures by following the proper ritual, may exercise control over supernatural beings. Men as well as gods may gain control over the mysterious forces of the world. Embodied and disembodied spirits may act and react upon one another, and a good deal of primitive religious practice, therefore, is concerned with following the technics of securing magical influence.

Gods are often conceived as more or less dependent upon man. They partake of the food offered to them in sacrifices. Hence, the Hudson Bay Eskimos deprive their spirits of food when they are displeased with them. Many African natives beat their idols and fetishes to punish them for misfortunes which they failed to prevent. Similar reactions to supernatural powers are sometimes exhibited by more advanced peoples. When the beautiful queen of Nepaul poisoned herself because her face had become disfigured by the smallpox, the king "cursed his kingdom, her doctors and the gods of Nepaul, vowing vengeance on all." He flogged and cut off the nose and right ear of the doctors, and then turned his attention to the gods, and "after abusing them in the most gross way, he accused them of having obtained from him 12,000 goats, seven hundredweights of sweetmeats, 2,000 gallons of milk, etc., under false pretenses . . . He then ordered out all the artillery, and when the guns from three- to twelve-pounders were loaded to the muzzle, he had them drawn up before the several deities. When the order to fire was given, many of the chiefs and soldiers ran away, panic-stricken, and others hesitated to obey the sacrilegious order; and not until several gunners had been cut down, were the guns opened. Down came gods and goddesses from their hitherto sacred positions, and after six hours heavy cannonading not a vestige of the deities remained." Here, indeed, was iconoclasm with a vengeance.

Primitive men, with their associated supernatural beings, may be said to be members of a common social order. Man's conduct in relation to his fellows falls under the head of morals; but his conduct toward his supernatural companions we call religion. In the latter the motive of fear plays a larger rôle, and the feelings of friendship and affection a lesser one, but notwithstanding these differences, primitive religion is essentially a social phenomenon springing from the same basic drives that determine the relations of man to other members of his community. Religious feelings and sentiments, like those which constitute man's moral sense, are woven out of the basic emotions that make man a social animal.

Primitive man is particularly anxious to keep on good terms with supernatural beings because of their uncanny power of expressing their displeasure in ways which cannot be foreseen or avoided. Taboos are scrupulously observed. Rites and ceremonies are conducted with meticulous care not to depart from the proper form of procedure. Customs having the sanction of supernatural approval are slavishly followed. The result is a uniformity of behavior and a social solidarity not found in more highly developed society. If a man commits an offense his gods may wreak vengeance, not merely on the man himself, but on his family or his tribe. "The savage," says Kropotkin, "obeys the prescriptions of the common law however inconvenient they may be. . . . His common law is his religion; it is his very habit of living. The idea of the clan is always present to his mind, and self-restriction and self-sacrifice in the interest of the clan are of daily occurrence. If the savage has infringed one of the smaller tribal rules, he is prosecuted by the mockeries of the women. If the infringement is grave, he is tortured day and night by the fear of having called a calamity upon his tribe."

Among primitive peoples religion powerfully reenforces tribal customs. The savage is controlled by the public opinion of both the natural and supernatural members of his group. His conscience is the voice of more than the tribal self; it is the voice of the tribe together with that of the even more to be dreaded supernatural beings who are very much concerned with tribal affairs.

As the ghosts of chiefs or other important personages evolve into gods, or when one god finally becomes the sole remaining deity, moral customs often come to be conceived as having sprung from one supreme lawgiver. When gods were numerous their moral characters were usually no better than those of mundane humanity, if as good. The gods and goddesses of the Homeric age were often cruel, revengeful, deceitful, and scandalously loose in their sexual relations. The Norse gods in Valhalla enjoyed to the full their bloodthirsty propensities in hacking one another to pieces, and became miraculously healed after each day's battle only to go at it again the next morning. And even Jehovah, as depicted in the early books of the Old Testament as a jealous God, clannish in his sympathies and ruthless in the exercise of power against offenders, meting out death for trifling offenses, and highly intolerant of freedom of religious worship, gradually improved in character in the Psalms and books of Prophecy, becoming a God of love and mercy, solicitous for the welfare of all peoples of the earth. Man, who makes his gods in his own image, improves upon his creations as he becomes more enlightened and humane. Man also makes his moral codes; then he generously gives the credit for them to his gods.

Since religion is a powerful aid in compelling obedience to the moral customs of the tribe, it acts as an integrative force that favors survival in the struggle of group with group. By and large, religions lend their aid to the enforcement of moral codes which sanction biologically useful kinds of conduct. As we have previously pointed out, however, these codes inculcate a certain amount of maladaptive behavior. This is inevitable because they are products of human thought and volition; and the vagaries of human thought might, and sometimes do, lead conduct very far away from useful channels. In fact one of the most potent causes of maladaptiveness in human conduct springs from belief in the supernatural. As Dr. Ritter has pointed out, there is much misdirected activity among savages associated with obtaining and consuming food, and many taboos as to what not to eat have no rational basis. The custom of sacrificing servants so that they can minister to a chief in the next world, the practice of suttee in India, the offering of human victims to secure good crops, to insure success in war or to avert epidemics, and many other forms of human sacrifices associated with religious rites, would seem to be far from advantageous to the groups that practice them. The acme of such waste of human life seems to have been reached by the Aztecs. "Scarcely an author," says Prescott in writing of the custom in Mexico, "pretends to estimate the yearly sacrifices at less than 20,000, and some carry the number as high as 50,000."

The belief in witchcraft has claimed its victims from time immemorial. Since witches are commonly conceived to use magic powers to accomplish malevolent purposes, the punishments directed against them have been unusually severe. The Laws of Hammurabi condemned witches to death as did the Roman Law of the Twelve Tables. In Exodus there is the express command, "Thou shalt not suffer a witch to live"—a command which, at a later period, was destined to be used to justify one of the most extensive and cruel persecutions of history. Curiously enough this great persecution occurred only a few centuries ago in the most enlightened countries of the world. Witchcraft had been severely punished throughout Christendom since an early period, but, for reasons we shall not attempt to discuss, the crusade against it was more vigorously carried on after the Renaissance and reached its acme in the fifteenth and sixteenth centuries. Witchcraft then terrorized people as never before. Lecky, who has given a vivid account of the subject in his *History of Rationalism in Europe,* tells us, "The clergy denounced it with all the emphasis of authority. The legislators of almost every land enacted laws for its punishment. Acute judges, whose lives were spent in sifting evidence, investigated the question on countless occasions, and condemned the accused. Tens of thousands of victims perished by the most agonizing and protracted torments, without exciting the faintest compassion. . . . Seven thousand victims are said to have been burned at Trèves, six hundred by a single bishop of Bámberg, and eight hundred in a single year in the bishopric of Wurtzburg. . . . At Toulouse, the seat of the Inquisition, four hundred persons perished for sorcery at a single execution. . . . Remy, a judge of Nancy, boasted that he had put to death eight hundred witches in sixteen years. The executions that took place at Paris in a few months, were, in the emphatic words of an old writer, 'almost infinite.' " Catholics and Protestants alike carried on the crusade with fanatical zeal. The doughty Luther joined in the fray in his usual emphatic fashion. "I would have no compassion on these witches," he exclaimed, "I would burn them all."

With the advance of science and the spread of education the craze slowly subsided. It was based on fear arising from a widespread belief in an ideology inherited from ancient times. More than mere traces of the same ideology are still with us, but they are rendered relatively innocuous because they are counteracted by other conceptions based on reason and sound knowledge.

While the efforts to extirpate the poor witches were at their height, the horrors of persecution for heresy had assumed proportions that far exceeded those of previous centuries. Like witchcraft this persecution had its basis in belief in the supernatural, but the dogmas involved were of a quite different character. Persecution for nonconformity to current religious beliefs and practices has, like persecution for witchcraft, prevailed widely among the peoples of the earth. An offense against the gods might bring retribution upon the whole tribe. The offender, therefore, must be treated with a severity commensurate with the magnitude of his crime. This policy, when not exceeding the bounds of moderation, might have some compensations in primitive communities as making for social solidarity. But the wholesale persecutions that raged in Europe during the Inquisition must have inflicted grave injuries upon the countries in which they prevailed.

That the barbarities of religious persecution should have increased to so remarkable an extent after the revival of learning is a phenomenon which, whatever its causes may have been, had its basis in the belief in eternal punishment that awaited the unfortunate individuals who espoused the wrong faith. From this standpoint no sin could be more heinous than the promulgation of doctrines that would lead others to eternal torture. The gentle Thomas Aquinas taught that if criminals may justly be sentenced to death, so much the more should heretics be killed to prevent them from spreading their dangerous opinions. Heresy, therefore, must be stamped out at all costs. The holy zeal with which ecclesiatical authorities caused the most diabolical cruelties to be inflicted on the adherents of other creeds during the palmy days of the

Inquisition is a perfectly logical result of the conviction that only through embracing the proper faith is it possible to escape from unending tortures in the world to come.

Consciously or unconsciously, religions tend to protect themselves from the disintegrative effects of doubt and schism by making it uncomfortable for the nonconformists. They are prone to deal with heresy as a political body deals with treason, and to a certain extent for much the same grounds. The survival of a religious organization is dependent upon the preservation of a certain uniformity of belief. For the attainment of this end acts are often resorted to that sacrifice the individual for the maintenance of uniformity of conviction. And by invoking punishments in the next world to be meted out against the nonconformists, a religious group is making a sort of defense reaction in the interests of its own preservation. During the Inquisition this sort of thing was grossly overdone from the standpoint of group welfare. Probably only to a minor degree was institutional preservation a consciously realized aim. The motives actuating inquisitors were doubtless partly vindictive and partly humanitarian, depending upon the individual participant. The effect of persecution when successful was to make for institutional preservation, though at a very considerable cost to humanity.

I can touch only briefly upon one other maladaptive effect of belief in the supernatural; namely, the theological opposition to the advancement of science. When natural causes were discovered for phenomena previously ascribed to supernatural powers, opposition to the new interpretation was inevitably aroused. The discoverer was viewed as a heretic endeavoring to undermine the basis of religious belief. Opposition to science was a part of institutional protection. The tendency to seek safety in the maintenance of the status quo is naturally strong in people who have never become accustomed to the idea of progress. But the tendency to oppose the progress of science is also strong in people whose religion is tied up with a cosmology with which science, as it advances, inevitably comes into collision. The cosmology accepted by the Christian world as divinely revealed in the Sacred Scriptures affords a striking example of this fact. As a result the conclusions of science that appeared to be inconsistent with this cosmology were stoutly opposed, and won their way to general acceptance (where they have done so) only after a painful struggle. This opposition has tended to retard scientific advancement and to deprive mankind of the benefits of scientific discovery and understanding.

The kinds of maladaptive conduct I have discussed as evils that can justly be laid at the door of belief in the supernatural do not prove that such belief has not, on the whole, exercised a favorable influence on morality. The general effect of religion upon the happiness and welfare of mankind presents an enormously complex and many sided problem. I can see little in most primitive religions which would be apt to contribute much to the happiness of the benighted creatures who believe them. They appeal chiefly to fear or to mercenary desires to obtain the necessities of life in man's struggle with his none too kindly environment. It is chiefly through terrorizing man that they compel him to observe the mores of the tribe. Here and there, indeed, even in primitive religions, we find expressions of kindly feelings toward the gods, but the dominant note throughout is that of fear.

It is only in advanced stages of the evolution of religion that the love of God, arising out of a belief in his goodness and love of his children, comes to be the dominant feeling in religious experience. The religious literature of the Christian world abounds in grateful testimonies of the joy and consolation derived from religious belief. This springs not only from the belief in eternal life, when friends and loved ones will be rejoined in an eternally happy existence, but also from a deep sense of peace and oneness with God that gives a more worthy significance to people's lives. Religious conversion often results in a happy release from torturing doubts and from a sense of sin, and brings a feeling of forgiveness and a conviction of God's approval that fills the convert with a strong desire to do good in obedience to God's will. The abiding sense of being accepted as a member of God's fold has its basis in the social emotions, but it exercises a peculiarly potent influence because of the alliance with a Being of infinite power and goodness.

The illuminating results of Starbuck's inductive study of conversion yield many evidences of this fact, as the following statements of the results of conversion will illustrate:

M.: I felt I belonged to a new category of being, nobler and more worthy to exist.

F.: Before, God had been far off in the sky . . . Now He was a tender, loving Father and very near.

M.: All at once light and peace came into my soul as gently as the sun coming up on a June morning. . . . I was embraced in the great plan of redemption. Provision was made for me, even me. I wept often that God should love even me.

F.: The change made me very affectionate, while before I was very cold to my parents.

M.: I felt it a duty to be polite and sympathetic. My enemies were changed to friends. My motive to chase riches was changed to that of saving others. I even made mistakes through altruism.

F.: I had more tender feelings toward my family and friends. I was no longer self-centered. The change was not complete, but there was a deep undercurrent of unselfishness.

Starbuck's study showed that most conversions occur in youth, the peak ages being thirteen and sixteen in girls, and sixteen in boys. Few conversions occurred after twenty. These young people, longing to love and to be loved, are in an emotional period of life, and frequently maladjusted and unhappy. Conversion often brings about a more satisfactory social adjustment and gives a freer outlet to more kindly emotions, the exercise of which is a source of greater happiness and peace of mind. The after-effects of conversion have, of course, varying degrees of permanency. Despite backsliding, Starbuck finds that "the persons who have passed through conversion, having once taken a stand for the religious life, tend to feel themselves identified with it, no matter how much their religious enthusiasm declines."

There are many kindly souls in whom a religion of love affords a powerful support to the good life. Even among the adherents of the horrible creeds accepted by Calvin and John Knox there were many good, devout people for whom the doctrines of hell and infant damnation figured much less prominently in their religious life than the sentiments of the Sermon on the Mount. The doctrines that were elaborated during the development of Christianity and which have led to the perpetration of innumerable cruelties, have tended to disappear, partly because of the general increase of enlightenment, and partly because people are becoming more humane. But as religion improves in character it also loses its hold. It has played a great part in the cultural development of the race. In all ages it has powerfully influenced the moral conduct of mankind. But the persistence of moral conduct of much the same general level under such exceedingly diverse religions as Christianity, Mohammedanism, Buddhism, Shintoism, to say nothing of many others, including groups of devout atheists, justifies one in the conviction that, however strongly religion may have acted to reinforce the altruistic impulses of human beings, morality will probably survive all changes in religious beliefs because, like religion, it is founded upon the basic human emotions and sentiments, and therefore will remain as long as man is man.

CHAPTER X

Some Controverted Questions of Right and Wrong

>   Wherever disputes arise, either in philosophy or common life concerning the bounds of duty, the question cannot, by any means, be decided with greater certainty, than by ascertaining, on any side, the true interests of humanity.
>   —DAVID HUME, *The Principles of Morals*

WHEN PEOPLE HOLD different opinions as to what is right or wrong, as they frequently do, they can often settle the question at issue in the same manner as they settle common disputes over matters of fact. When the disputants come to possess the same body of relevant data they may no longer disagree. For most disagreements of this sort, it matters little whether this or that standard is adopted so long as it is among those recognized by moralists as having a reputable standing. Many would doubtless exclude purely egoistic hedonism from such an approved list, despite the arguments which its adherents might adduce in its defense. Whether or not one deems that a teacher is right in administering corporal punishment, on occasion, upon some intractable offender, is not likely to depend on whether one is utilitarian, an intuitionist, or an adherent of the standard of self-realization.

In the great majority of cases peoples' differences over morals do not trace back to the different standards they may have adopted. There are, however, some exceptions. Kant declared "that to tell a falsehood to a murderer who asked whether our friend of whom he was in pursuit, had not taken refuge in our house, would be a crime." I think that the standards of few moralists would lead them to refuse to tell a falsehood to save the life of a friend. So far as the influence of standards on conduct is concerned, by far the most fertile source of disagreement is the ethics based on authority. In this ethics we find the final appeal is not to experience, but to some pronouncement alleged to emanate from God, or his accredited representatives, who are empowered to issue infallible decrees on matters of morals and religion. Back of these one cannot go. Being the final appeal, there is no ground for argument. Morals are thus subject to an ecclesiastical dictatorship more absolute than was ever imposed by any temporal sovereign. In so far as decrees have been issued, morals are fixed for all time. Whatever adjustments are required in a world of continual change can occur only in matters which were left out of account in the pronouncements hitherto made.

In an address on *Unchanging Ethics in a Changing World,* Father J. Ryan, in referring to the moral system of Christianity which has come down to us from its divine source, remarks that "God was looked upon as the foundation, the source, the guarantor, and the sanctioner of the entire moral code. All these ethical beliefs, all this ethical teaching, was laid down, explained, and enforced by living, active organizations. The answer to the question 'How ought I to live?' was clearly and authoritatively presented in the teaching of organized religion."

One who reads the above passage would hardly be prepared to find in the same address a sharp attack on "totalitarianism," which is designated as "the greatest menace in our present political life." The ethics defended is totalitarian, something laid down by infallible authority. To extend dictatorship over the field of morals and religion into the field of politics and government would be a perfectly logical step. At one time the Church claimed a certain jurisdiction in this field, which the force of circumstances compelled it to relinquish. The doctrine of the divine right of kings seems to have completely expired, with its last faint echo voiced by the late Kaiser Wilhelm. But the divine right of the Church to legislate in the realms it claims as exclusively its own, is still maintained as stoutly as ever. The effect would be to keep morals securely shackled along with its peculiar theological tenets. If an institution has the power of making rulings on matters of morals, which cannot be gainsaid, its hold upon all who accede to that claim is potentially stronger than any other allegiance. As a device for survival it leaves little to be desired. Institutions, like individual organisms, work for self-preservation, and the internal mechanisms making for the harmonious integration of their component parts play a highly important rôle. But an organism having the most effective internal integration must adjust itself to its external conditions. Too great rigidity in a changing environment sooner or later leads to extinction. An institution threatened by the impact of environmental changes naturally reacts by trying to mold its environment into conformity with its own life. This effort determines its attitudes toward new intellectual movements, the causes it champions, and its position on many controverted topics which have a bearing, even remote, upon its cherished doctrines.

In course of time, however, commitment to a rigid system, whatever advantages it may have possessed in keeping up a united front, may prove to be a source of weakness. An unchanging stand cannot be maintained on matters of science capable of definite establishment through methods of experimental inquiry. On such matters the Church has long since discreetly abandoned its attempts to lay down the law. In the moral sciences, in which conclusions cannot be established with a degree of conclusiveness that will convince anyone who will open his eyes and look, it is still possible to advance more or less plausible arguments in defense of traditional doctrines. But the advances in biology, psychology, and the social and moral sciences are carrying the battle into the field over which the Church has claimed jurisdiction, and making it increasingly difficult for it to maintain its stand. One cannot expect the Church to abandon its claim of infallibility on matters of morals and religion to which it is so deeply committed. The more probable result will be that its control of opinion will be insidiously undermined. Positions will be tacitly abandoned along with the retention of old forms and usages—keeping the outer shell intact along with a progressive weakening of control over the thoughts and conduct of its adherents.

It is much to be deplored that a great institution which has to its credit a long record of charitable works and devoted service to humanity, should still exercise an impeding influence upon the application of scientific methods in a field where they are most needed. This because it continues to stand resolutely for an authoritarian ethics and insists upon solving important moral problems by appeals to pronouncements instead of the methods of scientific inquiry.

The following subjects of discussion have been selected, not merely because there are decided disagreements over them at the present time, but because they so clearly illustrate the influence of general standpoints upon specific problems of moral conduct. In each case, when we seek the basic reasons for the opposed views, we find that they depend largely, and in some cases chiefly, on differences over the methods by which moral problems should be solved. On the one hand, we have appeals to some authoritative source; on the other, the positions taken are grounded on considerations of general welfare. Appeals to authority are also supported by arguments based on the probable effects of actions, but the final resort is to a divinely revealed command, or some *a priori* principle from which the right course of conduct can be derived. The truth of these statements will become more apparent as we proceed.

DIVORCE

Customs concerning divorce, like those in regard to marriage and all other matters having to do with the relations of the sexes, are subject to an extraordinary degree of variation among different peoples of the earth. Among the ancient Hebrews if a man married a wife and it happened later, "that she find no favor in his eyes, because he hath found some uncleanness in her," he could write her a bill of divorcement and pack her off without more ado; "And when she is departed out of his house, she may go and be another man's wife." But Jesus expressed a sharp disapproval of this practice as he did of the *lex talionis,* and other provisions of the Mosaic law. "But I say unto you, That whosoever shall put away his wife, saving for the cause of fornication, causeth her to commit adultery: and whosoever shall marry her that is divorced committeth adultery." Marriage, according to Jesus, made man and woman one flesh and, "What therefore God hath joined together, let not man put asunder."

The Christian Church regarded marriage as a sacrament and set its face firmly against plural marriage, concubinage, and divorce for any but the most serious causes, if at all. But where divorce for what was deemed adequate cause was not prohibited, the Church violently opposed the remarriage of divorced persons. It opposed the institution of civil marriage and endeavored to invest the marriage ceremony with the solemnity appropriate to a step of such great significance for the moral life. In speaking of the attitude of the Church toward the institution of marriage and the relation of the sexes, Lecky remarks, "There is probably no branch of ethics which has been so largely determined by special dogmatic theology, and there is none which would be so deeply affected by its decay."

The present changing attitudes on matters of sex have aroused widespread fear that our whole sexual morality is being undermined and is in danger of being swept away. The customary reaction of representatives of the Church is to endeavor to regulate the sex relations of individuals in accordance with Biblical texts or the pronouncements of ecclesiastical authorities. A typical illustration of this kind of reaction is furnished by the encyclical letter of Pope Pius XI on *Chaste Marriage*. As we might expect in *ex cathedra* utterances on morals or religion, it reiterates the stand taken by the Church in past ages. It quotes with approval the pronouncement of Saint Augustine to the effect that, "In the Sacrament it is provided that the marriage bond should not be broken and that a husband or wife if separated should not be joined to another even for the sake of offspring." It repeats the well-known sayings of Jesus on the indissolubility of marriage, and goes further, for even adultery shall not be considered a valid ground for separation. If there is any exception to the stability of marriage, however rare, "that exception," said the Pope, "does not depend on the will of men nor on that of any merely human power, but the divine law, of which the only guardian and interpreter is the Church of God." Even marriage in a state of nature such as might be contracted by savages, "is not subject to any civil power."

In giving the ground for the conclusion of the Church in

regard to the indissolubility of marriage it is best, I think, to quote the Pope's own words:

"If we wish, with all reverence, to inquire into the intimate reason for this divine decree, venerable brethren, we shall easily see it in the mystical significance of Christian marriage which is fully and perfectly verified in consummated marriage between Christians. For, as the apostle says in his epistle . . . to the Ephesians, the marriage of Christians recalls that most perfect union which exists between Christ and the Church."

Marriage, therefore, is not an ordinary event of nature; it is a transaction into which a supernatural element is somehow injected which sets it apart from the institutions made by man and bestows upon the Church the exclusive prerogative of its management. When a man marries he gets himself entangled in a contract sanctioned by God and which, therefore, he is eternally bound to observe.

The reasoning adduced to support the claim of the Church to exclusive control over an important sphere of human conduct could hardly carry conviction to anyone who is not willing to abrogate his right of private judgment and accept authority as his moral guide. That a policy so grounded should have led to undesirable results is no surprise. It has caused a divorced woman to be treated as a kind of social outcast who has forfeited one of the greatest privileges of life. The position of the Catholic Church and a considerable number of Protestant divines is that, no matter if she is not in the least to blame, she, being a divorcee, is thereby damaged goods. Were she to fall in love with a man with whom she could enjoy a happy home, surrounded by her children, her marriage could not be countenanced by Church authorities.

The immorality of this treatment of divorce, like the immorality of the treatment of heretics and witches, has its basis in supernaturalism. It is founded on a few sayings alleged to be inspired, and ecclesiastical pronouncements alleged to have been uttered under divine guidance. This method of settling problems of morals is a survival of the same method by which Galileo was proved to be wrong when he asserted that the earth moved. In matters of science it has been repeatedly proved that the position of the Church was wrong and the Church backed down. But in matters of morals there is no backing down. In this field when he speaks *ex cathedra* there is no possibility of a Pope ever making a mistake. Hence our morals must remain eternally in the grip of the dead hand of the past.

In this matter of settling questions of morals we have probably the most important issue that remains between science and theology. When the effort is made to determine what is right conduct in relation to divorce by digging up scriptural texts and the utterances of ecclesiastics, instead of basing the decision on considerations of human welfare, it is not surprising that the solution arrived at is repugnant alike to the spirit of humanity and to common sense. In proportion as we depart from rational and scientific methods of determining what is right and what is wrong, in that proportion will we have immoral solutions of moral problems. The world is growing away from reliance on dogma in ethics as it has done in the natural sciences. And reliance on dogma is as bad in the one case as in the other.

It has taken the world a long time to discover that really effective means of overcoming evils require knowledge of the reasons why the evils arise. This is largely because our concepts on ethics have been so little influenced by scientific modes of gaining insights and effective modes of control. It is only recently that we have begun to deal with the disorders of conduct from the broader viewpoint of causal understanding. In many cases great injustices are committed by rule of thumb methods based on the principle of this offense—this punishment. The method of forcible suppression not infrequently defeats its own end. It is claimed that granting divorce would prove an incentive to vice. But the opposite claim that making divorce exceedingly difficult would lead people to enter upon illegitimate unions, seems much more reasonable. Marital difficulties are so varied and involve so many different considerations that no simple set of rules can afford an adequate guide to just and humane decisions. Granting that the extent of divorce has become a serious evil, we need to know first of all what influences, social, economic, cultural, religious, or other, have conspired to bring it about. These questions may present many problems difficult of solution, but we cannot deal adequately with the situation until we have a much better understanding of it than is now possessed. The employment of women, their increasing financial independence, the growing urbanization of our population, the automobile, the movies, the influence of much of our current fiction, with its implication that irregular sex affairs are what is to be expected of people in the best society; the decline of religion, the falling birth rate, absorption in interests outside the home, and various other influences resulting from the development of our civilization, have probably all contributed to increase the evil.

To how great an extent the present high divorce rate is an evil is very difficult to determine. Those who are dismayed over the rapid increase of divorce seldom reflect upon the evils that would result if divorces had not occurred. How much unhappiness smolders under the lid is not regarded. The facts of separation are patent enough; they are matters of statistics which can easily be paraded to make an impressive showing and to create alarm over the impending decadence of all sexual morality. But the immoralities that are kept down, the abuse passively endured, and the anguish of slavery to brutal husbands, excite little sympathy so long as the lid is tightly clamped down and there is the outward seeming of respectability. These evils cannot be measured and made matters of statistics. There are, to be sure, many needless divorces resulting from little misunderstandings that might easily be patched up, as most of them are, in well-regulated families. But the great tragedy in matrimonial affairs is not so much divorce, as the marriages that should never have been made. But back of that is the still greater tragedy of the existence of brutal, selfish, and deceitful human beings among whom marriage is bound to be anything but ideal. So long as the world contains so large a proportion of individuals of these types, so long there will be many unhappy marriages. It is incredible that unhappiness would be diminished by making undesirable unions endure until death.

How divorce should be regulated is a very complex problem into the intricacies of which I have no intention of entering. To determine the way in which it should be solved would involve a consideration of the social and economic forces which have always been instrumental in shaping the customs of mankind in relation to mating and the perpetuation of life. In this respect the problem does not differ from numerous other moral problems with which we are confronted.

BIRTH CONTROL

Opinions on birth control, like those on divorce, depend to a large extent, although by no means exclusively, on whether or not they are derived from an authoritarian ethics. Here also the Catholic Church has made a ruling by which it is committed to an uncompromising opposition to this practice as against nature and essentially sinful. In his encyclical letter on *Chaste Marriage* the late Pope Pius XI states:

"No reason, however grave, may be put forward by which anything intrinsically against nature may become conformable to nature and morally good. Since, therefore, the conjugal act is destined primarily by nature for the begetting of children, those who in exercising it deliberately frustrate its natural power and purpose, sin against nature and commit a deed which is shameful and intrinsically vicious."

There being no scriptural text to serve as a guide, except perhaps the doubtfully relevant story of the unfortunate Onan, and since the subject failed to engage the attention of the Church Councils or the Fathers of the Church, contraception is adjudged a sin because it involves the "frustration" of a "natural power." But is the frustration of a natural power a sin *per se*? No one ever objected to frustrating the efforts of nature to fill his garden with weeds, and we continually frustrate the reproductive efforts of domestic animals by employing artificial methods of forcible control. Surely the Pope could not have meant that all frustration of nature's processes are wrong. On what principle, then, are we to decide as to which frustrations are right and which are wrong?

The Pope apparently was not opposed to the control of procreation, provided no unnatural means are employed, for he says:

"Nor are those considered as acting against nature who in the marriage state use their natural right in the proper manner, although on account of natural reasons, either of time or of certain defects, new life cannot be brought forth. For in matrimony as well as in the use of matrimonial rights there are also secondary ends, such as mutual aid, the cultivation of mutual love, and the quieting of concupiscence which husband and wife are not forbidden to consider so long as they are subordinate to the primary end and so long as the intrinsic nature of the act is preserved."

That intercourse between husband and wife is permitted for other ends besides generating offspring has been repeatedly stated by high Church authorities. In his booklet on *Birth Control,* which is issued with the imprimatur of Cardinal Hayes, Dr. John M. Cooper states that the marital relation is not only "lawful but it is in the nature of a strict right." And that "the refusal on the part of either party to grant the marital right constitutes a breach of contract, an injustice, provided, of course, that there be no serious or grave reason for the refusal."

Dr. Cooper is careful to explain that the Catholic position "does not hold that the married couples are under moral obligation to bring into the world the maximum number of children, to exercise no foresight or prudence, to bear offspring to the limit of physiological fertility, to labor for the maximum increase of the population, to bring 'an avalanche of babies'—all regardless alike of circumstances and consequences. . . . It does emphatically stand for chastity against artificial prevention of conception." But note the word "artificial." It was used advisedly, the implication being that the prevention of conception by natural means is morally permissible. He further states, "If they (husband and wife) elect to abstain during certain days . . . as, for example, the midmenstrual period, they are free to do so. Such abstention on the one hand places no unnatural obstacle in the way of procreation, and in the main is not open to the gravely harmful consequences that follow the use of direct contraceptive measures, and on the other hand may be fairly looked upon as a corollary of the general liberty to abstain by mutual consent when the parties so choose."

By way of supporting this statement as to the position of

the Church I will cite the opinion of another prominent opponent of birth control, Dr. H. G. Sutherland, who concedes that it is lawful, according to the teaching of the Church, for marrried people to limit intercourse to the so-called "safe period," a procedure which among other things is to be commended because "the sex love of the two people finds expression in a normal act, with which there is reason to think, certain physiological benefits are related." And further I may quote from E. R. Moore's book on *The Case Against Birth Control,* issued with the imprimatur of Cardinal Hayes, who supplies an introduction to the volume. Speaking of the safe period he says, "Morally its utilization with the hope of avoiding pregnancy is admissible."

According to these statements it is permissible for married couples to avoid pregnancy while enjoying the pleasures of marital rights over the greater part of oestrous cycle. It is now evident that it is not birth control *per se* to which the Catholic Church is opposed; it is merely birth control by artificial means.

In the controversies over birth control much has been written on the alleged damage to health arising from the use of contraceptives, the dangers of depopulation, the dysgenic effect of birth control, its bad moral effects on husband and wife, and various other unfortunate consequences into the pros and cons of which I shall not attempt to enter. These topics involve questions which can be answered only by scientific investigation. When sufficient evidence is available there is no reason why there should be any differences of opinion concerning them. As to the chief ends to be accomplished through birth control, there seem to be no valid reasons why Catholics, Protestants, Eugenists, and Birth Controllers might not agree.

That the perpetuation of life is one of man's chief moral duties, that it is justifiable to limit the family for economic, hygienic, and eugenic reasons; that people should not knowingly bring into the world, syphilitic, feeble-minded or deformed offspring, and that the marital relations of people should be conducted in a way that contributes most to their physical, mental, and moral well-being, are all matters about which enlightened people of all creeds have no need to differ.

These really important questions seem to be pretty well settled. It seems also to be pretty well settled to the satisfaction of high Church authorities that it is quite proper to restrict births by observing the so-called safe period, although nature is thereby frustrated in every oestrous cycle in the elaborate preparations she has made in vain for the implantation of a fertilized ovum in the uterus. The faithful, it appears, may now rest assured that it is quite right to get around Nature without too great a sacrifice of sexual enjoyment by an act of omission, although it is a "grave sin" to accomplish the same purpose by an act of commission. We have come down now to a rather fine point—a matter about as important as the moral distinction between tweedledum and tweedledee. How long will intelligent Catholics continue to be influenced by considerations of this trivial character?

But why, it may be asked, do leaders of the Catholic Church continue to make such a coil about a matter which, in the eyes of the most unprejudiced people, seems relatively unimportant if not puerile? In the early days of the modern birth control movement the idea of artificially controlling pregnancy came as a shock to conservatively minded people. It meant a willful interference with the divinely instituted process of generating life. Birth control was looked upon as fraught with grave dangers to population growth and sexual morality, and it therefore aroused the hostility of Catholics and Protestants alike. Its early founders were actuated by the humanitarian motive of relieving overburdened mothers in the lower income groups from the burden of large families, but it became apparent that much could be said for birth control from the medical, hygienic, eugenic, and other standpoints. The movement attracted to its standard large numbers of people of the highest intelligence and character, and its progress was so rapid as to effect in a very short time a decided change of attitude among the intelligent classes of the more advanced countries of the globe.

The attitude of the Protestant clergy gradually became more favorable and resolutions approving the proper employment of birth control were passed by the Lambeth Conference, the Federal Council of the Churches of Christ in America, an organization including over twenty-one million Protestant Church members, and several other religious bodies. Opinions on birth control in the Catholic Church could not fail to become liberalized as a result of the changing attitude of the intellectual world. The desirability of birth control for humanitarian, economic, eugenic, and hygienic reasons became too apparent to be denied. I strongly suspect that the position taken on birth control in the Pope's encyclical letter will eventually prove to be a source of embarrassment to his followers, who will regret his pronouncement without being at liberty to dissent from his infallible decree.

One very natural and justifiable cause of alarm was the fact that knowledge of contraceptive methods would inevitably be acquired by the unmarried and would therefore lead to an increase of illegitimate unions. The presumption of knowledge of safe periods also has its dangers. Since the publication of the Pope's encyclical letter, the control of conception by showing people how to take advantage of safe periods has been the theme of a number of Catholic books. Among these are *The Rhythm,* and *The Sterile Period in Family Life,* both printed with ecclesiastical approval and sold to young and old alike. Through disseminating the information conveyed in these volumes, the sexual morals of youth may be undermined as much as by the birth controllers who are held up to scorn. The issue, it seems, is no longer over birth control; it is simply over method. As Margaret Sanger remarks, "It comes down to a safe contraceptive or a safe period and that is about where both sides stand now."

Birth control is sometimes right and sometimes wrong. When it is right and when it is wrong are vastly more important than the particular means by which it is brought about. It has great possibilities for good or for ill and it should be employed in such a way as to contribute most to the happiness and welfare of those directly concerned and also their posterity.

EUTHANASIA

It is sometimes the unfortunate fate of human beings to suffer unspeakable agonies without hope of relief. Here is a patient with her face almost eaten away by a cancerous growth that compels her to lie and suffer in agony for the few remaining weeks, or months of her life. Though the patient, as such patients sometimes do, may implore the doctor to end her useless suffering by a painless death, the doctor, if he complied with her request, would be legally guilty of murder. In such cases surreptitious acts of mercy are sometimes done. But physicians are loath to make themselves liable to be tried for murder, and they frequently allow patients to die in lingering agony when it is perfectly clear that death is the greatest boon for which the sufferer could hope. Dean Inge has remarked, "It seems anomalous that a man may be punished for cruelty if he does not put a horse or a dog out of its misery, but is liable to be hanged if he helps a cancer patient to an overdose of morphia!"

There is a widespread sentiment in the medical profession in favor of making euthanasia legal. As a result of many conversations on the subject I find that the natural reaction of intelligent and humane persons, who approach the proposal with an unbiased mind, is one of approval. The general sentiment in favor of euthanasia is growing. The societies for the legalization of euthanasia in England and the United States number among their members many of the most prominent intellectual leaders of these countries. Euthanasia represents a humanitarian measure based on the unselfish motive of relieving useless pain. There is scarcely any movement one could name that is more unequivocally based on motives of pure philanthropy.

Obviously the right to take life under any conditions should be adequately safeguarded. In the law proposed in the State of New York, an individual over twenty-one years of age who is suffering from an illness pronounced incurable by his physician can petition the Court to be given a painless death. The Court then appoints a commission of three persons, two of them being physicians, to pass upon the case; and if their report is favorable, euthanasia may be administered by any person chosen by either the patient or the commission.

The humane sentiment which has effected the abolition of torture, even of the worst criminals, is endeavoring to terminate the continuation of torture in hopeless individuals who long to escape from their sufferings. No one would be so callous as to wish for the continuation of their life. Their dearest friends are glad when their sufferings are finally relieved by death, but it is the thought of taking life that gives one pause. The natural reluctance to take any active part in the termination of another's life, however much it would be desired for the sake of the sufferer, prompts people to find grounds for opposing such actions. Among the reasons advanced, apparently the most influential one is based on convictions concerning the relation of man to his Creator. For some, the command, "Thou shalt not kill," settles the matter once for all. Life, it is said, is sacred, a gift from God, and only God has the right to take it away. We human beings are in this world to fulfill the purposes of our Maker, and even if we have to bear the pains of an incurable malady which incapacitates us for any useful work, we are carrying out some part of God's inscrutable plan, and we have, therefore, no right to desert our post. In other words, they also serve who only lie and suffer.

Euthanasia has often been opposed on the ground that it would form a precedent which might lead to abuses. G. K. Chesterton, who drew quite liberally on his imagination as in writing his entertaining fiction, warned us that euthanasia, "at present a proposal for killing those who are a nuisance to themselves, but soon to be applied progressively to those who are a menace to other people," is but an entering wedge that will open the door to all sorts of intolerable evils. Mr. H. G. Sutherland tells us, "Once let loose the principle of legalized killing, and its application would inevitably widen with every year that passed." But the principle of legalized killing is already legalized in capital punishment and has been so for a long time without having been extended in the least in its sphere of application. In fact its application has shrunk very considerably since the days when people were hanged for stealing a few shillings.

The alarmist attitude that a good measure might come to be abused is a common obstacle to reforms of many kinds. We have to trust to the common sense, sympathy, and fairness of people to keep us from all sorts of intolerable abuses. The practice of euthanasia may be widened beyond the very restricted application now proposed, but if so, it will be limited by the same considerations of human welfare and justice upon which we must rely for the preservation of any of our rights and privileges.

To withhold the benefits of euthanasia because of the possibility that cures may sometime be discovered for ills that are now fatal, would be to prolong agony in nearly all cases for the sake of a false hope. Sometimes diseases are pronounced incurable from which the patient eventually recovers, but only very rarely would a case of this kind be a willing candidate for euthanasia. People die every day from the mistakes of doctors, and it is possible that a patient might be painlessly put to death who otherwise would have recovered. There are many kinds of illness about whose fatality doctors can be quite certain, and it would be mainly in cases of this kind that they would take the responsibility of advising euthanasia. After all, in this matter, as in other things, gains must be balanced against losses. And there can be little doubt that the losses would be infinitesimal compared with the gains.

Unfortunately the merciful endeavors of the friends of hopeless sufferers are probably destined to be thwarted by the opposition of those who rely upon alleged supernatural authority for the basis of their morals. Sometime, we may hope, the opposition will weaken until it is no longer strong enough to intimidate legislators. In the meantime our incurables must continue to suffer their useless pains.

THE OPPOSITION TO ANIMAL EXPERIMENTATION

Another moral problem upon which the opinions of many people are strongly swayed by emotion and often supported by an appeal to an ethics based on authority, is presented by the persistent opposition to experiments on animals carried on in the effort to check the ravages of disease. The regard for animals and the resentment aroused by any wanton cruelties inflicted upon them are worthy of all respect. These sentiments form the chief basis of the antivivisection movement. I need not remind the intelligent reader of the great debt which humanity owes to the researches of Pasteur, Koch, Roux, Ehrlich, Metchnikoff, Banting, von Behring, and other great investigators whose experiments on animals have led to dramatic achievements in the conquest of disease and the alleviation of human suffering. The experimental methods employed by these and other investigators have been attacked on the ground that it is intrinsically immoral to inflict pain on innocent animals for the sake of human gain. This is the moral question involved.

As to the factual aspects of the controversy, we find it concerned with two issues: (1) the amount of pain inflicted, and (2) the extent of the benefits resulting from the experiments. On the one hand, it is contended that the amount of pain suffered is relatively small, while the results obtained have been of enormous benefit to men and animals alike. On the other hand, there is the claim that great numbers of animals are subject to unspeakable cruelties and that the benefits derived are of relatively little or no value. I shall not enter upon the details of this controversy. As to the training, knowledge, and competence to evaluate the issues involved, the two parties are scarcely comparable. The antivivisectionists have the advantage of readily appealing to the sympathies of lovers of animals by tales of wanton cruelty inflicted by hardened vivisectors. This side of the argument is presented with much exaggeration and gross misrepresentation. Having come in contact with a considerable volume of antivivisectionist literature and having spent many years in close association with laboratories in which animal experimentation is carried on, I find the usual portrayal of the cruelties practiced almost incredibly grotesque. As to the slight benefits conferred by experiments on animals, the claim is too absurd to require refutation. It is chiefly of interest as indicating the extent to which opinions can be warped by fanatical devotion to a cause.

The foregoing issues hinge largely on matters of fact. But as the question is one of morals, the attempt is sometimes made to decide it on the basis of assumed moral principles. According to Anne Kingsford, an ardent opponent of vivisection, "That which is morally wrong can never be scientifically right." Miss Line-af-Hagely, in a lecture on antivivisection, declared, "I do not believe that it is right to do wrong in order to obtain some physical advantage," and then devoted most of the rest of her lecture in trying to show that vivisection has resulted in no real benefits to mankind.

The assumption here and in many other similar statements seems to be that the universe is so constructed that an act intrinsically wrong simply cannot be productive of good results. The wrongfulness of the act is first determined independently of its consequences and then it is inferred that its consequences must square themselves with the moral judgment. This is a common viewpoint in popular thinking on questions of morals. Suppose we start with the proposition that it is wrong to inflict pain upon a defenseless animal. Unless we appeal to some *a priori* principle or command, we must conclude that it is wrong to inflict the pain because of the injury to the animal, but if it is a surgical operation from which the animal would benefit later everyone would approve the act. But suppose that a part of the consequences of the act was the acquisition of knowledge that would increase the well-being of numerous other animals, we should logically have to take these consequences into consideration quite as much as the benefits to the animal itself resulting from a bit of surgery. If the morality of an act is determined by its consequences, we should not take account merely of some of the consequences and ignore the others.

I suspect that opinions as to right and wrong on this and similar problems may be influenced to no small degree by adherence to some *a priori* principle assumed to have general validity. Popular maxims such as, "Two wrongs never make a right," and "Good never comes out of Evil," are often invoked as a guide in making moral decisions. Since as commonly employed they involve begging the question, they tend to prevent moral judgments from being based on considerations of general welfare.

THE ETHICS OF BELIEF

In W. K. Clifford's writings on ethics, which are characterized by a freshness, originality, and boldness which sets them sharply apart from the usual prosaic disquisitions on this subject, there is an essay on *The Ethics of Belief*. It begins with the story of a man who owned a ship about to set sail with a number of emigrant families. The vessel was old and probably not seaworthy, and its owner was very unhappy over the thought that she ought to be thoroughly overhauled and repaired. But this would involve much expense which he was loath to incur. Wishing to quiet his conscience, he said to himself that she had made many trips and never had a mishap and surely she would return safely after this one. "He would put his trust in Providence, which could hardly fail to protect all these unhappy families." He finally persuaded himself that the emigrants in his vessel were entirely safe and felt no further uneasiness concerning their fate. The vessel went down with all on board; "and he got his insurance money . . . and told no tales."

This man was certainly responsible for the death of the people who embarked upon his vessel. Although he may finally have become perfectly sincere in his conviction that his vessel was safe, he convinced himself by an illegitimate and immoral method. He had no moral right to believe as he did on the basis of the evidence before him. He arrived at his belief by taking an unfair advantage of the infirmities of his own nature and made his reason subservient to his own selfish desires.

Clifford's story of the owner of the unseaworthy boat illustrates a widespread attitude toward questions of fact. People are prone to bamboozle themselves into believing what they like to believe. They willfully close their minds to evidence against their views. They eagerly and uncritically accept as true whatever supports their opinions, and they even deny the truth of anything that is inconsistent with them. These intellectual immoralities are common. They make it difficult for wrong opinions, once acquired, ever to be dislodged from the mind. If these opinions make a strong emotional appeal, or if they have been instilled in early life and become deeply ingrained in habits of thought, they usually persist in face of any amount of adverse evidence.

People are much more cognizant than they were a generation ago of the tyrannical influence that emotion exercises over reason. This is evinced by the frequency with which one encounters the phrase "wishful thinking." Propagandists are not slow to take advantage of the fact that if you want to convince people you should make your main appeal to their emotions instead of their intellect. One of the chief aims of education is, or rather should be, to make people cautious in coming to conclusions, always ready to give a fair consideration to opposing arguments, and willing to abandon conclusions when the balance of evidence turns against them. Always to keep a candid and open mind goes sorely against one's natural inclinations. We are by nature partisan-minded; that is a part of our traditional clannishness. It is a great wrench to give up an opinion that we have fondly entertained and perhaps defended with warmth. Instead, we usually prefer to cherish our illusions.

But rail as one may against the pigheadedness of the rank and file of humanity, no one of us is anywhere near being free from emotional bias in forming his opinions and especially in defending them. Unquestionably the advancement of science has done much to encourage the spread of the scientific habit of mind. The investigator must obey the canons of the scientific method if he would be successful in the discovery of truth. He cannot allow himself to be unduly influenced by his desires and prejudices or any form of wishful thinking. He must treat his hypotheses as means of discovering truth, which are to be put aside whenever they prove to be unsupported by facts. But the mental attitude essential to the discoverer of truth should be cultivated by people in all walks of life. Everyone needs to base his conduct on what is true instead of what is false. Hence a wholesome skepticism is an intellectual virtue which everyone should cultivate as a preventive of falling into error.

To any properly educated person all that I have said is commonplace enough, and need not have been said at all. But to the great majority of people it is not adequately realized, and by many it would be rejected as a dangerous and subversive doctrine. I admit that it is subversive, but only of doctrines that cannot stand the test of critical examination. Whatever is true has nothing to fear.

For long ages the world has been taught that credulity is a positive virtue. In matters of religion, especially, unquestioning belief was extolled as one of the chief merits of a true Christian.* To doubt was one of the worst crimes, if it

---

* In speaking of his successful efforts to preserve his faith, the genial Thomas Browne states in his *Religio Medici*, "I can answer all the Objections of Satan and my rebellious reason with that odd resolution I learned of Tertullian, *Certum*

concerned matters of religious faith, and worthy of the severest punishment in this world and an eternity of torture in the next. Mohammed was equally hard on the unbelievers: "The curse of God, and of angels and of all men, under it they shall abide forever, their torment shall not be assuaged" (Koran, XCVII). Palgrave relates that when Abd-el-Lateef was preaching to the people of Riad, he referred to the legend that Mohammed prophesied that his followers would divide after his death into seventy-three sects, seventy-two of which were destined for Hell and only one for Paradise. When Mohammed was asked by what signs the fortunate elect could be recognized, he replied, "It is those who shall be in all conformable to myself and to my companions". "And that," added Abd-el-Lateef, in an impressive voice, "that, by the mercy of God, are we, the people of Riad."

This kind of doctrine was quite typical of Christian sects during most of the Christian era. If belief in the right doctrine is necessary for salvation, those who are firmly convinced that they alone hold the true faith will naturally be intolerant of all doubts. Unbelief, being the worst of all possible sins, must be put down at all costs. With so many sects claiming a monopoly of the tenets necessary for salvation, the question of how to make a right choice becomes too important to be left to the fallible reason of the individual. He might err and also lead others to perdition. It is therefore the duty of those who are firmly persuaded of the truth of their own opinions to stifle free inquiry and to inculcate the attitude of unquestioning credulity. Children should be brought up in the true faith by taking advantage of their

---

est, quia impossibile est. I desire to exercise my faith in the difficultest point;" there being no merit in believing where there is sufficiently reasonable grounds for so doing. In dealing with the mysteries of religion, upon which he loved to ponder, he endeavored to school himself "to believe a thing not only above but contrary to Reason, and against the Arguments of our proper Senses."

early susceptibility to persuasion. Any method whatever that will keep them in the fold is abundantly justified.

Under the influence of such creeds it is scarcely to be expected that a sane and reasonable ethics of belief could prevail. No scientist would claim that there is any special merit in believing something that seems highly probable, or in doubting something for which there is no good evidence. Many religious fanatics, on the other hand, look upon unbelief in certain religious doctrines as indicative of bad character. In several of our states an atheist was formerly ineligible to testify in court, the assumption being that he would probably not tell the truth. Not believing in God, however conscientiously he may have come to his opinion, the atheist must therefore be a bad man.

We have our beliefs and our doubts on all sorts of subjects without considering that the least praise or blame should attach to any of our opinions. Belief and doubt have no merit *per se*. It is wrong to believe without evidence, and it is our duty to doubt when the evidence is insufficient. Otherwise we should be betrayed into error; and erroneous opinions are a poor basis for conduct.

From this standpoint it is morally wrong to inculcate opinions on highly controversial topics into the minds of children by taking advantage of the ready suggestibility of their immature minds. Our own opinions may be wrong, and the child should be given a fair chance to form his own without being biased in advance. Whether the doctrines inculcated are political, economic, or religious, the uniformity of opinion brought about by instilling them into the uncritical and unsuspecting minds of the young, saddles them with a burden of many errors whose elimination will be all the more difficult because they are accepted mainly on non-rational grounds.

These common violations of the ethics of belief spring to a

considerable degree from the motive of institutional preservation. Catholics insist strongly on bringing up children in the faith and instilling their beliefs into them before they can judge of their truth or falsity. This of course makes for institutional stability, although by unfair means, which are doubtless considered as justified by the end achieved. Incidentally, any errors involved in the teaching thus perpetuated are insured against being dislodged from the minds of those who believe them. Intelligence is a disruptive force which is always a menace to the stability of any doctrine that is built upon a shaky foundation. Its free exercise is always dangerous to uniformity of belief, unless the belief is sufficiently well-grounded to stand on its own merits. Efforts to protect beliefs from the devastating effects of criticism are therefore apt to be made wherever it is held that important social, economic, or religious institutions are thereby endangered. The right of free thought and free speech have been acquired only after a long struggle, and they are still far from being adequately recognized even in the freest countries. Those who attempt to restrict these rights may be actuated by good motives, but in their fear of permitting their opinions to stand or fall as a result of critical discussion they are adopting a shortsighted position that only impedes progress. If truth is what we genuinely desire to see established, whether or not it conflicts with our opinions, we must maintain those conditions under which truth can most readily prevail.

The attitude of the dogmatically minded is that we have the truth. Those who are opposed to us only disseminate error. Therefore their opinions should be suppressed. But no one really knows that he possesses the truth. No true scientist would offer the least objection to having his hypotheses critically tested. He welcomes free inquiry and criticism. Many of his beliefs are purely tentative, like his hypotheses. But when we come to matters of morals, politics, and religion, the scientific attitude as to what should be believed is far from generally adopted. Yet does not the discovery of truth in these fields involve the same methods of thinking that are employed by the astronomer and the biologist? And have we not, therefore, the same reason for encouraging freedom of thought and expression in the one case as in the other? One of the most formidable obstacles to progress in the present chaotic state of the world lies in the failure to recognize the beneficent influence of free thought and free speech. Those nations which have so ruthlessly suppressed intellectual liberty in the interest of a self-seeking nationalism or a fanatically embraced ideology are only sacrificing their future welfare for present dubious objectives.

But, it may be asked, are we not obliged to believe many things the evidence for which we are not in a position to evaluate? Surely we cannot be supposed to examine into the grounds for all the propositions we hold to be true. All educated people believe that the sun is somewhere near ninety-three million miles distant from the earth; that Jupiter is many times the size of our own planet, and that water is composed of hydrogen and oxygen in a two-to-one ratio, although very few persons could give the reasons upon which these conclusions are based. No one doubts that Washington crossed the Delaware or that Caesar crossed the Rubicon. Do we not accept most of the things we believe on faith? And are we not entirely justified in so doing?

The answer to these questions must be unhesitatingly Yes. We are almost compelled to accept most of our beliefs on authority if we are to get along at all. But is this accepting them without evidence? Certainly not. It is accepting them on the basis of confidence in the statements of other people who, we have reason to think, are better qualified than we are to have an opinion. I may be unable to check up on the calculations by which the astronomer estimates the remoteness of the sun from the earth, but all the data are available so that anyone who qualifies himself can verify the conclusion. Many astronomers have verified it. So far as I can judge, they have no particular interest in lying about it. The conclusion fits in with an organized body of knowledge which I have reason to believe is mathematically precise. On the basis of such knowledge astronomers predict the occurrence of an eclipse of the sun many years in advance, telling us to the minute when it will begin, how long it will last, and specifying the parts of the earth in which it will be total. Maps are sometimes published in the newspapers showing what these areas are. Everyone can verify the predictions of the astronomers as to the time and duration of the eclipse. All of these facts give one a high degree of confidence that the astronomers know what they are talking about. Although I take their statements on authority, I am really basing my conclusion on evidence.

When I accept statements on the authority of astronomers, chemists, historians, or scholars in any field, I cannot, of course, be sure that I am right, but I would be less apt to be wrong than if I attempted to form conclusions from my own very limited knowledge. I may not credit all the statements, even of astronomers. When I read that the universe is expanding at a certain rate I am rather dubious, especially since some astronomers do not share this opinion. The proper attitude for me, as a poor ignorant layman, is one of skepticism, and not one of either affirmation or denial. I am quite ready to accept most of the statements of Livy in his writings on Roman history, but when he relates, in all seriousness, that after Marcus Curtius plunged on horseback into a chasm that had opened in the Roman Forum the chasm immediately closed, I am more than skeptical.

When one accepts facts and conclusions on authority, as any well-trained investigator would, he does not surrender in the least his own right to judge for himself. Ordinarily one would be foolish if in a case of illness he did not place more confidence in the opinion of a competent doctor than in his own judgment, but if the doctor's diagnosis seemed too absurdly improbable he would rightly refuse to accept it. In basing our opinions on the judgments of others we are simply relying on probabilities to the best of our knowledge. Following authority in this way is quite different from the acceptance of authority in which the mind of another is the final court of appeal. The authority that insists upon the abject surrender of private judgment has no place in science or any other field of critical scholarship. Whether or not it has a legitimate place in relation to morals and religion is a mooted question. If I believe that a book is divinely inspired throughout and literally true, I must, in consistency, accept every proposition in that book, improbable as it may seem to my unaided judgment. And if I am further convinced that Popes and Church Councils speak with divine authority on matters of morals and religion, I must likewise subscribe to everything they say on these subjects. In speaking of the Roman Church, Cardinal Newman states, "She makes it imperative in everyone, priest and laymen, to profess as revealed truth all the canons of the Councils, and innumerable doctrines of Popes, propositions so various, so notional, that but a few can know them. What sense, for instance, can a child or a peasant, nay, or any ordinary Catholic put upon the Tridentine Canons, even in translation? . . . These doctrinal enunciations are *de fide;* peasants are bound to believe them as well as controvertialists, and to believe them as truly as they believe that our Lord is God."

But if I grant all this, my surrender to authority is conditioned upon the reasons by which I am led to regard the authority as authoritative. Since the acceptance of the basic doctrines in question involves the adoption of a lot of opinions on matters of both theoretical and practical importance, I am under an unusual moral obligation to be cautious, critical, and unbiased in adopting my fundamental tenets. Were I to allow myself to become convinced of the truth of a number of abstract theoretical propositions purely on the basis, say, of an emotional upheaval at some religious revival, I would be guilty of a real sin against the cause of truth. Even if these propositions were true, it would be wrong to believe them for such a reason.

Clifford makes the statement, "Religious beliefs must be founded on evidence; if they are not so founded, it is wrong to hold them." This may strike the gentle reader as a bit Puritanical because he may think it justifiable to entertain a religious belief if he derives comfort and consolation from so doing, even if the belief is false. This raises the question as to whether it is right to practice autodeception for one's own personal ends. If you assume that always and everywhere it is wrong to deceive, then the question is settled. With all due respect for the virtue of veracity, I do not see how this assumption can be proved. Under most circumstances it is doubtless wrong to deceive, and hence there is a certain presumption against the morality of trying to convince oneself of a religious doctrine that is not supported by evidence.

In making this statement I am not forgetting the mystics whose sublime contemplations are believed to give them direct intuitions of truth. Doubtless their unusual experiences seem very convincing to them. Personally I cannot see how anyone who has read William James' *Varieties of Religious Experience* can interpret these experiences as the mystics have usually done. Fortunately the perplexing subject of mystical experience I have no need to discuss. If people have truths mysteriously revealed to them they are, of course, justified in believing them. If they are deceived, they form conclusions from what appears to them perfectly valid evidence.

CHAPTER XI

The Ethics of Enmity

IN THE CHAPTER of his *Principles of Ethics* on "The Confusion of Ethical Thought," Herbert Spencer clearly showed that throughout human history mankind has followed two diametrically opposed codes of conduct which he calls the "ethics of amity" and the "ethics of enmity." To many persons the expression "ethics of enmity" may seem to imply a contradiction in terms. We commonly associate amity with goodness, and enmity with evil. The mere suggestion that enmity has a useful function, with an ethics appropriate to it, is apt to arouse at once an inimical reaction. Nevertheless, probably ninety-nine out of every hundred who profess allegiance to an ethics based exclusively upon amity would, if their country were invaded by a hostile army, pay scant attention to the maxim "Resist not evil," and would wholeheartedly support measures for inflicting death upon their adversaries. They would do this, moreover, in obedience to the dictates of conscience and in the conviction that failure to support the cause of national defense would be base and highly blameworthy.

Up to, and in some countries within recent times dueling, as Spencer points out, was supported by the strongest moral sanctions, and a man who failed to challenge one who insulted him was looked upon as a coward and a poltroon. Our code of honor befitting a gentleman has changed. We are no longer under a moral obligation to fight duels, but on occasion collective fighting meets with almost universal approval. Nearly everyone would concede without hesitation that the Belgians were morally justified in forcibly resisting the ruthless and unprovoked invasion of their country in 1914. Under the circumstances, according to the recognized moral standards of mankind, right conduct for the Belgians called for the employment of the ethics of enmity rather than amity toward their foes.

In treating of the ethics of enmity I am concerned not with what conduct is right in the best of all possible worlds, but in the present very imperfect conditions of human life to which we perforce have to adjust ourselves. If we are in the midst of a war that has been unjustly inflicted upon us, it will profit us little to declare that war is an evil and that it is wicked to engage in it. We may concede that war is a great evil and that nations should endeavor by all honorable means to avoid it; but when a country is in the throes of a life or death struggle, its citizens must adjust themselves to a real emergency. If I were attacked by a pack of wolves I would feel that it would be quite ethical to kill as many of these animals as possible. From the standpoint of the wolves, cooperation in the common cause of attacking my person is highly commendable behavior, the kind of behavior which nature has compelled these animals to follow under penalty of dying of starvation. Since I am under an equal necessity of resisting the wolves, we both espouse the ethics of enmity in our dealings with one another.

When we look out upon the world of living creatures we find numerous instances of different species whose interests are essentially antagonistic. The brown rat and the black rat are keen competitors, and now the one and now the other prevails. Man is attacked by numerous parasites and other maleficent creatures which we deem it quite proper to treat as enemies. We would bestow the highest commendation upon any one who succeeded in exterminating the hookworm, the blood fluke, or the pallid spirochete. But there are numerous people who believe that our conduct would be morally wrong, that "all life is sacred" and that no living creature should be willfully put to death. Numerous Brahmans, Jainists, and Buddhists of India sincerely endeavor to extend the ethics of amity to all sentient creatures whatsoever, and large numbers of them die annually from the bites of cobras and other venomous snakes. The costly practices of these Hindu sects are the consequences of simply carrying out the ethics of amity to an extreme though logically consistent degree.

Aside from the membership of the religious cults referred to, there is a very general agreement that the good life requires, on occasion, the treatment of other peoples as enemies. This obligation naturally involves killing or incapacitating as many of the enemy as is necessary to attain security. As to the infliction of incidental injuries upon noncombatants, or at least those not participating in the support of military operations, a host of moral problems arises which presents great difficulties of solution in accordance with any general principles of procedure. These problems vary greatly according to the methods of warfare that are employed. Inevitably much hardship, and even death, is inflicted on numerous civilians as a part of the larger end to be attained. And the extent to which considerations of mercy are allowed to have weight depends in part upon the methods employed by the enemy. In the late World War neither side made use of poison gas, not so much because of any hesitation on humanitarian grounds, as because each participant did not wish to expose its inhabitants to the retaliations that would follow.

Many attempts have been made to reach international

agreements in the aim of mitigating the barbarities of war. Despite numerous infractions of these agreements with which each party has accused the other, there has been, up to the present century, a slow progress toward making war less inhuman. These efforts to combine an ethics of enmity and an ethics of amity have inevitably been fraught with many inconsistencies. According to prevailing standards, humanitarian considerations cannot be allowed to stand in the way of attaining the chief military objectives. One must not give aid or comfort to the enemy, even by allowing food to be sent to hungry children, if more food might thereby be available for the enemy forces, or aid, directly or indirectly, in carrying on the war. We may greatly deplore making cripples of innocent women and children who take no part in the conflict, but under conditions of modern warfare this is simply inescapable and we have to reckon it as a part of our larger moral obligation. We might be willing to forego *some* of the advantages conferred by our weapons of war if we could thereby save those whom we have no desire to injure, but how much? Certainly not enough to involve an increased loss of our own force that would imperil the success of our cause.

Our traditional treatment of the ethics of enmity has been characterized throughout by muddled thinking and futile sentimentality. Along with a general approval of the practice of enmity, and high praise of those who take part in it, there has gone a refusal to concede that it has any moral justification. Typical attitudes are saturated with hypocrisies which result from closing the eyes to inconsistencies which people are unwilling to recognize.

The extent to which duty requires us to be humane to our enemies presents many problems which differ much according to circumstances and, as in other moral problems, the conclusions arrived at will be influenced by the general moral philosophy to which appeal is made. The doctrine that the duty of the state is to acquire power, that since the state is the supreme arbiter on matters of morals it can do no wrong, and that anything that makes for the power of the state is therefore right, easily lends itself to the condonement, if not the encouragement, of all sorts of atrocities if they are thought to conduce to the attainment of power. The deliberate employment of the policy of *Schrecklichkeit* to terrify the enemy, and the systematic brutalization of the youth of a nation to imbue them with the hatred and cruelty which such a policy requires, is a logical consequence of the power ideology. The persuasion that gangsterism is the natural and proper rôle for a strong nation to pursue has received a rude jolt as a result of the Second World War, but it would be too optimistic to conclude that it is safely disposed of.

Efforts to make war less inhuman, which had previously been making some progress, have not borne conspicuous fruit during the last few decades of our history. This is owing in part to changing methods of warfare, but it is also owing in no small measure to the resurgence of gross brutality and disregard of all considerations of justice and humanity in the treatment of enemies and subject peoples. The deliberate mass murder, starvation, torture, and fiendish cruelty inflicted on multitudes which run even into the millions, could have been carried out only by a people deliberately brutalized in accordance with an ideology which recognizes no moral obligation except to the state as the embodiment of power. This striking revelation of the diabolical possibilities of human nature must come as a shock to those accustomed to thinking well of their kind. And it must be a bit disconcerting to optimists in general to reflect that, in spite of its great advances, our civilization has just seen some of the darkest pages of its history.

In addition to the ethics of employing violence in wartime, there is the matter of adherence to the normal standards of veracity. In general, certain conventions such as the immunity conferred upon the bearers of the white flag, and promises to interrupt hostilities for a period, etc., are usually respected. On the other hand, efforts to deceive the enemy by conveying misinformation or causing him in any way to draw false conclusions are among the approved measures of good strategy. A soldier who fell into the hands of the enemy would doubtless feel it incumbent to lie like a trooper if he thought he could deceive his captors as to the state of his own forces. If it is right to kill your enemy, why should one hesitate to lie to him? Even in peaceful relations the obligation to be truthful is often considered more binding between friends than between strangers, especially if they are somewhat unfriendly. During the peacetime rivalries of nations, the willfully misleading statements of diplomats range from slight misrepresentations to the downright lying so liberally employed by Adolf Hitler. In general, I think the verdict of most people as to lying would be, in wartime, Yes; in peacetime, No. Both, however, with certain reservations due to very exceptional circumstances.

When war is followed by peace the ethics of enmity are not completely abandoned by states but are continued as preparations for war, ostensibly defensive, but often with the intent of aggression. If one nation prepares for war, other nations are led to do the same for the sake of their own security. Then there are rivalries for the acquisition of more territory, trade routes, concessions, and opportunities for the exploitation of more primitive peoples whose labor and resources may be employed to enrich the dominant state. These economic rivalries are common provocatives of war, especially where the different nations have a stake in the same region. In many instances the extent to which there is resort to violence without a declaration of war may assume considerable proportions, as recent history has shown.

The development of organized groups within states leads to many kinds of loyalties, with their many correlated kinds of enmity. Where the interest of one group is opposed to the interest of another, or is believed to be so, whether it really is or not, enmities frequently arise which result in violent action. The most important of these antagonistic groups are those of employers and employees. Laborers band together in order to secure fair wages and proper working conditions which they have only too much reason for believing would not otherwise be granted; and employers band together to resist the demands of labor. The result is commonly decided in one way or another by the party having the stronger power. On the theory espoused by Marx and his followers, the interests of capitalists and laborers are entirely opposed, and the laborers should adopt the ethics of enmity and dispossess the employing class. Accordingly, at all times the paramount duty of the proletariat is to carry on the class war. As stated in the *Communist Manifesto:* "The Communists . . . openly declare that their aims can be attained only by the forcible overthrow of all existing social conditions. Let the ruling class tremble at a communistic revolution." The atrocities committed in liquidating the bourgeoisie during the Bolshevik revolution proved the seriousness of the grim warning.

The class war, as the communists endeavor to mold it, extends beyond national boundaries. The methods by which it should be fomented and carried out are clearly set forth in *The Program of the Third International* adopted in 1928. It is a carefully prepared program of war in which the communists are advised that "when the revolutionary tide is not rising" they "must advance partial slogans and demands that correspond to the everyday needs of the toilers and combine with them the fundamental tasks of the Communist International." Later when the propaganda has sufficiently done its work and the party is strong enough to secure the leadership of the working classes, it will embark upon its revolutionary enterprise of overthrowing the existing social system. In order to achieve this end it is necessary to widen class distinctions, intensify class antagonisms, and create an organized and disciplined group, antinational in spirit, and obedient to a centralized control.

This disruptive movement derives its strength from the prevalence of economic injustice and the existence of economic maladjustments, such as widespread poverty and unemployment, in a land of abundant wealth and productive power. It has developed an ethics of its own, which, like other group ethics, centers in the perpetuation and extension of its power. Its avowed objectives are humanitarian and it commands a sort of religious devotion among its numerous adherents, who feel that they are engaged in a crusade to effect the liberation of oppressed humanity. And they manifest a particularly virulent antipathy to other reforming groups who are not convinced of the superior efficacy of the communistic system.

Persistent antagonisms occur in varying degrees between many kinds of intranational groups, due to differences of race, religion, politics, or other interests, but the hostile acts to which they occasionally give rise are rarely the deliberately planned result of a definite ideology. Employers and employees constitute groups whose interests are in part opposed in that they are competitors for the products of labor and management, but they are not entirely opposed. The conflicting interests are often exaggerated in order to create a sentiment of class solidarity among the workers. In our present economic order employers and employees are in large measure mutually dependent, although this fact has not prevented capitalists from compelling labor to work for starvation wages. Both are advantaged by an increase of total wealth, even though the capitalists may receive much more than their due share.

The great technological advances of the last century have resulted in increased wealth and the cheapening of many articles. The dollar watch was typical of many products which are purchased by all classes. Partly as a result of more efficient production and partly on account of the rising power of labor to enforce its demands, real wages in most industrial countries have risen to a noteworthy degree. Hours of labor have been shortened, conditions of labor have been improved, and many other advantages have been secured. Although it may be to the advantage of an industrial employer to get as much done as possible for the lowest pay, this does not follow to the same extent for the interests of employers as a class. If the wages of the great mass of workers are so low that they cannot afford to buy anything beyond the barest necessities of life, producers lose a very profitable market for their goods. Also, if labor is compelled to work very long hours, its efficiency is impaired. It is also important to employers to maintain safe and wholesome conditions for their laborers and so far as possible to retain their good will. All of these considerations vary greatly with circumstances, but they show that relations of employers and employees are not entirely antagonistic, but involve, like so many relations in both the individual and the social organism, a combination of competition and cooperation. There is competition for the surplus values of labor; there is cooperation in the production of this surplus. How the surplus should be divided in an equitable manner is an essentially ethical problem into which a great variety of considerations enter; and the problem would remain if capitalism were eliminated and the state became the sole employer.

A general guiding principle which is widely accepted as an ideal is: "From each according to his powers; to each according to his needs." Although like many other general formulations it may require qualification, as various commentators have pointed out, it represents a notable approach toward an ideal objective. Unquestionably we are far from this goal and we cannot get very close to it without drastic modifications of our present economy. No one can deny that many of our most urgent problems of human welfare are economic. Recognition of this fact has been painfully slow. It has long been ignored by writers on ethics. And economists, until the last few decades, so far as they have treated of the human aspects of their science, have occupied themselves largely in explaining how the iniquities of the economic order are the inevitable consequences of immutable laws of production and distribution of wealth.

Professor J. A. Hobson has remarked in his able volume on *Economics and Ethics* that "it is not difficult to understand how the doctrine of a natural economy inspiring a policy of complete *laissez faire,* a free play of economic forces without political or other let or hindrance, satisfied the rationalistic humanitarians of the nineteenth century and stemmed the tide of ethical criticism which revolutionary socialists, or literary and artistic idealists brought against the workings of the economic system."

After all, the economic system is, to a considerable degree, automatically therapeutic in its workings. But its inherent *vis medicatrix naturae* has proved to be hopelessly inadequate to cope with the maladies that have accompanied its rapid mushroom growth. Our economic system is a new kind of organism, the like of which has never before appeared in human history. From the biological standpoint it is not surprising that it should develop a good many internal disorders and that it should require a good deal of doctoring to enable it to function passably well.

Hobson remarks that:

"Insensibly, the dominant conception of the conditions of organic unity is coming to prevail. . . . the new tendency to assimilate all wholes or unitary systems, from the atom to the universe, mental as well as physical wholes, to the structure and behaviour of an organism, and to see them all as systems of inter-acting parts with internal inter-relations on the one hand, and external inter-relations with other similarly constructed wholes, upon the other, is exceedingly germane to our thesis. For it establishes the inseparability of the economic activities in men or groups of men, from the other activities which these organic beings display in all operations concerned with the production and utilization of economic or marketable goods. Not merely do economic and non-economic activities incessantly interact in every process, but the 'good' or 'satisfactions' got out of every set of activities can only be interpreted in terms of the organism as a whole."

If we make comparison between human society and an organism, it should be on the basis of functional coordination rather than structural analogies. The individual organism is a system of coordinated elements in which needs and performance are pretty closely adjusted in accordance with the principle of supply and demand. In the organism there is competition due to the tendency of its several parts to assimilate and expand, but it is held in check by counterbalancing influences which are automatically set into operation. This is rendered possible through the reaction modes of the component elements which, like the specific instincts of social animals, have been molded in the course of evolution for the proper performance of their respective rôles.

Normally, the cooperative activities within an organism are carried out in admirable harmony and precision. They automatically correct their own maladjustments. At times there may be abnormal hypertrophies, dystrophies, or functional atrophy; or groups of cells, as in a malignant growth, may follow the ethics of enmity, liquidating surrounding cells, literally as well as figuratively, by means of their proteolytic enzymes. As a rule, however, the organism does a perfectly wonderful job of cooperative construction and maintenance. To a large extent this achievement is an automatic product of the supply and demand relations which are often manifested in very complex and indirect ways in the formative and regulatory activities of the organism, as they are in the economics of human society. Egoism of component parts is essential to the life of the individual, but the task of subordinating it and making it contribute to the general weal has been accomplished for each organism only through the accumulation of successive trials extending over many millions of years.

In fitting animals for life in social groups, nature has adopted the device of rewarding altruism with egoistic satisfactions, as is exemplified in the pleasures derived from maternal ministrations and various social activities. But there are other ways in which a similar result is arrived at more directly. In accordance with the teachings of the classical economists, the egoistic pursuit of wealth results in social benefits. Competition naturally leads to diversity of occupation, but the new lines followed must supply a social demand, else they would receive no reward. Supply and demand tend to settle down into a fairly stable equilibrium without any consciously directed control. There are many reasons, which I shall not attempt to discuss, why the natural economic adjustments have failed to work out and have led to the anomalous conditions of competition and the development of subordinate group egoisms standing in varying degrees of inimical relationships. One of the many indictments against our economic order is its tendency to engender enmities. The conflicts of workers and employers are often injurious to both participants and interfere with the interests of the general public. The results, when securing greater rewards for the working classes, may in the end be conducive to the general welfare, but the method is costly.

The various group rivalries within a nation raise many perplexing moral problems. By common consent, war between nations justifies conduct quite opposed to that which is approved in times of peace. But there are various gradations between the organized conflicts of nations which we call war, and for which there has developed a certain system of rules, and many other kinds of rivalry. Where group is pitted against group within the nation, there is a strong tendency for each group to give moral approval to almost any conduct that conduces to success. This is often exhibited in the writings of the proponents of the "class war." It was conspicuously exemplified in practice during the Russian Revolution. How far this tendency is justified in the various gradations in the conditions of group rivalry, is a question fraught with unlimited worries for the moral philosopher.

The ethics of enmity presents a much larger problem than the ethics of war. It cannot be decided by setting up a sharp distinction between war and other kinds of conflict. A sharp distinction does not exist. As to intranational group rivalries, the general sentiment would be opposed to the kind of violence employed in war, except in the case of justifiable revolution. The authority based on force might be used to destroy groups, but not their members, in dealing with such nefarious organizations as the Silver Shirts and the Ku Klux Klan. As organizations they are eligible for the application of the ethics of enmity.

If one would endeavor to picture the work of a "functional society," in the sense in which this term is used by Mr. Tawney, as "a society which aimed at making the acquisition of wealth contingent upon the discharge of social obligations, which sought to proportion remuneration to service . . . which inquired first, not what men possess, but what they can make, create or achieve," it would be a society run very much after the pattern of the individual organism whose component parts have made such a striking success of harmonious cooperation. How far in our striving for the creation of an ideal social organism we can take lessons from the unconscious cooperative achievements of the living body, is a question that may be well worth pondering. For many of the similarities observed in the integrative behavior within the body and between the bodies constituting the social groups, spring from the common properties of life. The individual organism normally rewards its laborers for performing their functions well. And through an essentially democratic cooperation it turns egoistic functioning to good account by the institution of automatic checks and balances which subordinate it to the welfare of the whole. This is a part of "the grand strategy of evolution." A society *tends* to do the same thing, but it succeeds only in ways that are relatively imperfect and clumsy and wasteful of much energy in internal friction. Much unsubordinated opposition is inevitable, not only because its individual members are intelligent and free, but because the character of the group is subject to continual and extensive change. Opposition ranges from friendly rivalry to bitter enmity, and it is prone to transgress its normal functioning and become pathological, especially when it assumes a violent form. In the imperfect state of the world which has thus far prevailed, however, many conflicts have been the means of avoiding greater evils. When, where, and to what extent conflict should be engaged in, are typical questions concerning the ethics of enmity which a peace-loving people may not willingly face, but a failure to take a realistic attitude toward them might prove to be a grave sin of omission.

After all, from a comprehensive view the ethics of enmity and the ethics of amity should have a common aim. But whether this is taken to be the welfare of humanity in general or some other objective, a multitude of further questions immediately press for solution. All these I shall discreetly avoid, contenting myself with the foregoing brief discussion of a mainly uncharted field presenting many perplexing problems upon which there is much disagreement and much thinking made quite irrational through the influence of emotion.

CHAPTER XII

The Justification of War

> International politics is essentially a competitive struggle for power between sovereign members of State systems. War is an incident of this struggle.
> —F. L. Schuman, *International Politics*

> But war's a game, which, were their subjects wise, Kings would not play at.
> —William Cowper, *"The Winter Morning Walk"*

THE DIVERGENT OPINIONS on the justification of war have had little relation to fundamental ethical theory. Those guided by an ethics based on authority, as well as the adherents of other systems, differ widely among themselves as to the morality of war. Some have endeavored to settle the question very simply by appealing to the commandment, "Thou shalt not kill." Many of the early Christians tried to live according to the maxim, "Resist not evil," and refused to perform military service. A number of the early Christian Fathers opposed all participation in warfare. But this attitude did not last long. As the Christian Church grew in power, its policy as to war adapted itself to the usages of the times. Saint Augustine definitely justified war under certain conditions and Saint Ambrose attacked the doctrine of nonresistance and condemned those who did not oppose willful aggression. War came to be officially approved by the Church, as is exemplified by the Crusades. Bishops led troops in action, and cardinals planned and instigated aggressive warfare.

For most Christians the pacifist attitude derived from the Gospels became an impractical ideal. It was generally conceded that if everyone were kindly disposed toward everyone else and refrained from molesting his neighbors, we would all get along very much better, but there is always the wicked other fellow who is continually stirring up trouble and against whom it is necessary to take repressive measures. By the common consent of nearly the entire Christian world, wars of defense are morally justified. And almost every country endeavors to convince its people that its own wars are wars of defense. Even the most shameless aggressions are excused by the claim that they were necessitated by the unendurable provocations of the enemy. People will always fight better and more willingly when persuaded of the justice of their cause.

If we concede that defensive wars are morally justified, we must admit that it is not always easy to decide when a war is really defensive. Frequently provocations occur on both sides, and the people of each country are sincerely persuaded by propaganda that the other country is solely to blame. Where there are international rivalries for trade, spheres of influence, and other desired objectives, the determination of war guilt may be a matter of much difficulty. Nations, like individuals, struggle for the means to live, and it is only natural that in the pursuit of their aims they commit many infractions of peaceful relationships. There being no higher court of appeal, the only way in which nations could settle their grievances in the last analysis has been to resort to arms. For this reason, most nations are more or less exposed to the alternatives of war or the humiliating endurance of injustice. Extreme pacifists assert that always and everywhere the latter is the better course. Under no circumstances, they maintain, is it permissible to resist one's enemies, be the provocations what they may. The relatively small number, even among pacifists, who take this position commonly justify their standpoint by what they consider to be the teachings of Jesus. But, as was contended by Grotius in his great treatise on *The Law of War and Peace,* we know very little concerning what the attitude of Jesus toward war really was. As to the relations between individual men, his teachings were predominantly pacifistic, even if on one occasion he drove the money-changers out of the Temple. He did not grapple with the problem of warfare between states, nor with the ethics of political relationships. His ethical teachings dealt with the relations of individual man to man and of man to God.

The question in which the adherents of a naturalistic ethics are chiefly interested, however, is not the basis from which the policy of nonresistance is deduced, but how this policy will work out in practice. Will the rigid adherence to the principle of "Resist not evil" advocated by Tolstoi, for instance, really prove feasible? It might work, of course, if everyone followed it. But in the absence of all forcible means of protecting life, liberty and property, when thieves, bullies and rascals of all descriptions are free to follow their own bent without fear of retaliation, would not conditions soon become intolerable? Tolstoi had no fear of such a result; Mr. John Haynes Holmes apparently shares this attitude. Just refrain from all violence and the aggressors will sooner or later see the error of their ways and cooperate to bring about an era of peace, and good will will eventually reign. I fully recognize the force of good example, as is illustrated by the nice little stories in Mr. Holmes' *New Wars for Old,* but I cannot convince myself that the elimination of all resistance to violence in this wicked world is likely to bring many sinners to the mourning bench.

War, though an evil, is not the worst of all evils. Should a country submit tamely to an invasion of barbarians? Was it wrong to turn back the tide of the Huns? Are nations never justified in rising up and throwing off the yoke of the oppressor? One cannot tell what would result if nations went all the way in the direction of nonresistance and allowed all other peoples to come in and do as they pleased without fear of being checked by force. Few people, I fancy, would like to be inhabitants of a country which tried the experiment. But if one does not adopt the ultrapacifist position advocated by Tolstoi and J. H. Holmes he must face the problem of when and where violence must be employed. This problem cannot be solved by appealing to a maxim. Whether war is right or wrong would then depend upon the circumstances of the individual case. Once we abandon the position of the extreme pacifists, we are driven to consider the pros and cons.

I assume, then, that there are certain wars which are morally justifiable. Whether or not war is an institution of permanent value as a means of racial improvement or material and cultural advancement, is a radically different question upon which opinion has been far from unanimous. In general, war is not defended just for its own sake, although its virtues have not infrequently been extolled. I suspect that this has often been done in order to surround it with a glamour that helps to conceal the more sordid motives that were its real inciting cause. Frederick the Great declared, "War opens the most fruitful field to all the virtues, for at every moment constancy, pity, magnanimity, heroism, and mercy shine forth in it," whereas peace leads to sloth, selfishness, cowardice and degeneration. Whatever the motives may have been which prompted this statement of the habitually hypocritical Frederick, there have been many similar utterances made with entire sincerity. Even kindly

John Ruskin, who maintained that "war was the foundation of all great art," stated in speaking of the game of war, that "the great justification of this game is that it truly, when well played, determines who is the best man; who is the highest bred, the most self-denying, the most fearless, the coolest of nerve, the swiftest of eye and hand. You cannot test these qualities wholly, unless there is a clear possibility of the struggle's ending in death." But the war which Ruskin extolls is an idealized contest, not "modern war, scientific war, chemical and mechanized war, worse even than the savage's poisoned arrow," and he concludes with apparent regret, "perhaps . . . any other kind of war is impossible now." He was doubtless right.

It is undeniable that there is some truth in the statements just quoted, although the true picture is more somber than the ones painted. The chief objections to war are familiar to all. The loss of life, the sufferings of the wounded, the permanent crippling of soldiers, the ravages of disease, which often cause more deaths in the civil population than the army; the wanton destruction of property, the rape of women, and the hardships, fears, humiliations and brutalities endured by the populations of invaded countries, are all evils which the most ardent militarists do not even attempt to deny. More recently we have become aware of the mental damage that is suffered by the participants in war and the demoralization that follows wars in the civil population. The people of militaristic states commonly lose, to a greater or less degree, the intellectual liberty which is so essential for the higher cultural life. This last consequence of war is rarely given due weight by the militarists, or even by the pacifists. Intellectual liberty is a precious and hard-won acquisition whose curtailment cannot fail to constitute a formidable impediment to progress. The Goddess of Liberty always takes a back seat in the presence of Mars.

But the wartime restrictions of liberty carry over into times of peace, especially in those countries in which peace is only a sort of armistice to be employed in making further preparations for war. In Germany during the Hitler regime the Press became merely the cowed and servile creature of the dictatorship in peace as in wartime. Representative government was virtually abolished. The schools were made centers for the inculcation of patriotism and national antipathies, in order to further the militaristic aims of the government. Germany, once a leader in all fields of scholarly endeavor, has shown a marked deterioration in her intellectual productiveness and the activities of her higher institutions of learning. Her youth were regimented, disciplined and brutalized in the aim of fitting them to carry on war in a manner to inspire terror in the hearts of their enemies. The moral damage suffered by her population is perhaps the worst of the evils which her policies have brought upon her.

In considering the alleged value of war we should distinguish between the conflicts of primitive peoples and those of modern industralized states. I have already alluded to the process of group selection resulting from intertribal warfare. There can be little doubt, I believe, that group conflict has tended to develop the virtues of courage, loyalty, veracity and mutual aid within the limits of the belligerent organization. At a more advanced stage of culture war has been a means of welding smaller groups into larger and larger units. Professor E. A. Ross states, "Warfare has been the great state maker." Groups band together for common defense and are often united by conquest. So long as men are divided into small tribes, there can be little progress in the arts; trade is limited; ideas are restricted to a narrow field; there can be little division of labor, and hence anything more than a primitive industrial development is impossible. No great projects such as road-making, canal-digging, or the erection of large buildings can be accomplished. Cultural life must stagnate on a crude level. The conflicts between larger units bring peoples into contact with other cultures. Many new things are learned and the intellectual horizon is widened. It is only in the fairly large state that culture attains a high degree of development. As Steinmetz declares, "Ohne Krieg kein Staat."

One may concede the force of these arguments for the past benefits of war and maintain that in our present stage of development these same benefits would not be obtained, or at least whatever benefits might result would be greatly outweighed by the damage suffered. We certainly no longer need war for the exchange of ideas or the formation of large national groups. The argument that war is a "biological necessity," a means of eliminating the weaklings and enabling the fittest to survive, may be countered by the statement that, as a matter of fact, war eliminates the best of the breed and spares those unfit for military service. The proponents of war have often appealed to the teachings of Darwin, as affording a justification of war on biological grounds. But the conclusions they commonly draw from these teachings are quite different from those drawn by Darwin himself. The only statement I can find in Darwin's writings bearing on modern warfare is the following from *The Descent of Man:* "In every country in which a large standing army is kept, the finest young men are taken by the conscription or are enlisted. They are thus exposed to early death during war, are often tempted into vice, and prevented from marrying during the prime of life. On the other hand, the shorter and feeble men, with poor constitutions are left at home and consequently have a much better chance of marrying and propagating their kind." Apparently, therefore, Darwin regarded the biological influence of modern war as distinctly bad.

There is, I believe, little doubt that this statement holds true of most wars among modern civilized peoples. Unquestionably many wars have been important factors in aiding the expansion of victorious racial stocks, as is exemplified by the remarkable spread of the people of Anglo-Saxon lineage over a considerable part of the globe. But in the wars of recent years, especially among European states, the defeated peoples were not greatly reduced in numbers and have often increased more rapidly than their conquerors. Besides, victory often depends much more upon mere size, material advantages, helpful alliances, and other factors having no close relationship with the innate qualities of the participants. Under these conditions the fortunes of war are not likely to promote racial improvement. Selective elimination does not always result in advancement; in fact it often leads to degeneration. The kind of change it effects depends upon the circumstances under which it acts. One may be a strict orthodox Darwinian and maintain with entire consistency that, under present conditions, war is an evil of the very first magnitude.

Most apologists for war on biological grounds concede that its influence within a nation or people is dysgenic, but that, in leading to the survival of a people having superior endowments, its net influence results in progressive development. If under present conditions it does not work out in this way, one might contend that this is because the victors do not make the proper use of their opportunities. Nations habitually pay little attention to the possible biological effects of their successful wars. They are much more concerned with boundaries, indemnities, economic opportunities, and other matters in which genetic values do not figure.

From the purely biological standpoint, the most effective kind of warfare was that carried on by the Children of Israel who frequently exterminated all their rivals without regard to age or sex. Since biological evolution occurs through the successive replacements of somewhat different genetic stocks, a people believing in the high general level of their inheritance might readily become convinced that they should supplant inferior brands of the human family and run no risk of being outbred by them. As I pointed out somewhat over twenty-five years ago, many German writings, before and during the First World War, contained pleas that victory should be utilized to promote the increase of the German people by dispossessing the inhabitants of conquered areas and settling them by Germans. As stated by Klaus Wagner: "It is a great and powerful nation which overthrows a less courageous and degenerate people and takes its territory from it. . . . The great nation needs territory. Therefore it must spread out over foreign soil and must displace strangers with the power of the sword."

The persuasion that other peoples are human material of an inferior sort, who should be replaced by those of superior Aryan lineage, has apparently grown apace between the two world wars. The doctrine of the native superiority of Teutonic stock has elicited a very considerable volume of adverse criticism. Opposition to it has doubtless been intensified by its incorporation into the Nazi philosophy. Probably for this reason, together with others, there has been a growing sentiment against the conclusion that the races of man differ in any really important characteristics. There can be no doubt that many of the arguments for Nordic superiority are unsound. Average differences in intellectual capacity and emotional reactions are more difficult to demonstrate beyond all cavil than was formerly supposed. On the other hand, it is difficult to show that such average differences do not exist, or that they are not important. Arguments on this topic are seldom advanced without bias, and bias as to racial characteristics that results in action may produce very unfortunate results, as we have recently seen. If important race differences should be indubitably proven to exist, they would afford no moral ground for inhuman treatment. They might be given consideration in applying measures for the control of population growth, if they should prove to have an important influence upon the direction of biological evolution. But this moral problem involves too many unknowns to be discussed with profit at the present time.

In the preceding discussion I have been concerned with the influence of war as a selective agent. Mere loss of life, while an important biological effect, is irrelevant from the broad evolutionary standpoint. The evolutionary significance of war depends upon how it affects the relative net reproductive rates of genetically different stocks. This problem, which I have considered more at length elsewhere, has generally received an oversimplified treatment. The books of D. S. Jordan, for instance, while containing much valuable material, almost completely ignore the very important aspect of group selection which has been emphasized, especially by several German writers. Viewed purely as a problem of evolutionary biology, one must consider the relative effects of both individual selection and group selection. From this standpoint the case for the evolutionary value of war is certainly far from sufficiently clear to make warfare a moral duty which we owe to future generations.

The great moral problem of our attitude toward war involves consideration of a wide range of effects besides those on the biological level. Many of these are so obviously bad as to require no discussion. Wars may, of course, bring wealth to a victorious people. They have often done so in the past. The prospect of gaining wealth and power has afforded a potent incentive to war to the present time. Nations fight to promote the material and cultural advancement of their own peoples, and convince themselves that they are striving for a worthy end. The welfare of other peoples concerned is not given consideration, often on the ground that they are deemed not so important anyway. Whatever may be said for this kind of warfare in the past, it has recently been proved to be more destructive to all parties concerned. That war from the economic point of view never pays, even for the victor, as contended by Norman Angell, may have been a doubtful thesis. At least it probably has been so to date. With greatly increased power of destruction, and with the promise of further increase in the near future, warfare between the leading nations of the world would be economically suicidal in addition to its greater evils in other ways.

The destructive possibilities of war have now assumed such colossal proportions that the moral problem of finding peaceful solutions of international disputes has become the most urgent with which the world is faced. Will the moral resources of man prove adequate to the task? After the First World War, the nations of the world demonstrated their moral incapacity to meet the situation. The obligation to succeed is more imperative now. But with the representatives of all the nations concerned clearly convinced of this fact and sincerely desiring to avoid war, the attainment of this end, with all the rivalries with which nations are engaged, is still a ticklish business which Mars may be contemplating with a cynical grin.

CHAPTER XIII

Our Expanding Moral Horizon

An individual man, to be harmoniously great, must belong to a nation. . . . Affection, intelligence, duty, radiate from a center. . . . What is wanting is, that we should recognize a corresponding attachment to nationality as legitimate in every people, and understand that its absence is a privation of the greatest good. —GEORGE ELIOT

Magnanimity in politics is not seldom the truest wisdom; and a great empire and little minds go ill together.
—EDMUND BURKE, *On Conciliation with America*

AS MAN ADVANCES in the understanding of his world the sphere of his duties becomes more widely extended. According to the notions of the moral life once very prevalent, a man who is honest, kindly and conducts himself with scrupulous rectitude in his personal dealings, and withal cherishes a sentiment of becoming piety, has reached about the acme of moral perfection. Ideas of moral goodness have been slowly growing away from such a conception. The demands of the good life now place less emphasis upon personal qualities and more upon one's obligations as a member of a social group. These demands require one to be concerned with what is wrong with the world, how the wrongs came to exist, and what can be done to set them right. Hence there arises the duty of understanding one's world, first of all, as an indispensable means of making it better. And one is led to grapple with world problems to the best of his ability, because they affect the welfare of every individual.

Peoples have accepted the social order into which they are born, much as they accept the order of nature. Woodrow Wilson has stated:

"Yesterday, and ever since history began, men were related to one another as individuals. . . . To-day the every-day relationships of men are largely with great impersonal concerns, with organizations, not with individual men," and this, he continues, is "nothing short of a new social age, a new stage setting for the drama of life."

The realization that social institutions are the creation of individual human beings, and that they can be modified better to fulfill man's needs, brings with it a much broader conception of the range of one's duties. If institutions are made by man, they are a part of his responsibilities. When they fail to work well, man has the power to change them unless he has suffered himself to become too completely controlled by the products of his own creation. To avoid this not uncommon fate may require eternal vigilance, but it is one of the chief duties that fall to man's lot as the responsible source of his social order. The preservation of freedom is of paramount importance in relation to matters of social morality because without it peoples are powerless to change the institutions under which they live.

When man attempted to adapt his social order to his needs he embarked upon a truly formidable task, or rather a series of tasks which are subject to continual change. The many political, economic, and other disorders of the organization of society which call for remedy present varied problems with which the moral rules concerning personal relationships are inadequate to cope. They are analogous to the varied disorders of the body which arise from different causes and require different kinds of treatment. To determine what is right to do in the case of social evils requires much the same type of procedure as that followed by the physician in his endeavors to promote the health of his patient. Dealing with social ills requires, like dealing with the disorders of the individual body, a knowledge of just what is wrong and why. In both cases the great need is causal understanding. Understanding may, and often does, point the way to the discovery of effective remedies. But failing in this, it may afford means of greatly reducing many evils through methods of prevention.

In dealing with so extensive a topic as social disorders and the proper moral conduct in relation thereto, I must limit myself to a very few aspects of the theme. I might elaborate at length upon the evils flowing from the unequal distribution of wealth and the enormous waste of productive activities in our present economic order. The poverty, hardship, ignorance, ill health and distorted lives consequent on economic maladjustments present a problem of social morals whose importance and urgency cannot be too strongly emphasized. The subject has been amply discussed by many writers. Besides, its adequate treatment would require a whole book.

One of the important evils with which our society is sorely afflicted and which may be regarded as in part one of the devil's brood engendered by economic maladjustment, is our large volume of crime. Various estimates of its cost in money are almost incredibly large. Our efforts to cope with it have thus far resulted in almost complete failure. A long prevailing aim in dealing with crime, which finds expression in the *lex talionis,* was to administer punishment in proportion to the offense. This was in accordance with the traditional formalistic conception of morality as involving a sort of debit and credit account, in which entries on the debit side could be erased by suffering the proper amount of punishment. This might take the form of a certain fine, or so many years in jail, or later in purgatory. Then the account is squared. These notions still prevail, although the old motive of retaliation in punishment has largely given way to the more kindly aim of reforming the criminal. Unfortunately, however, punishment, at least as usually administered, generally fails to achieve this purpose. In speaking of prisons, H. E. Barnes remarks, "Instead of reforming the criminal they are in reality institutions for the training of more effective and determined criminals."

In some instances the application of better reformatory procedures has met with an encouraging degree of success. More, however, may be expected from measures of prevention based on studies of the actual influences which have led to criminal careers. These studies have shown that a great deal of crime springs from other social evils which are still flourishing. Hence the prevalence of crime does not present an isolated problem, but one that is closely interwoven with many others: economic, legal, educational, hygienic, psychological and genetic. Any great amelioration of the situation will probably have to wait upon accomplishments in other fields.

Much has been written on the high proportion of defects, both physical and mental, of the criminal class. The world is full of damaged souls which have been spoiled somehow in the making, and they form a fertile recruiting ground for the criminal population. Many of them are afflicted with hidden physical ailments which have robbed them of ambition and hope and shriveled up their capacities for enjoyment. Many suffer from maldevelopment of their emotional life that distorts their mental vision, upsets their normal balance, and causes them to behave in all sorts of aberrant ways. Many develop in undesirable directions as a result of lives of want and hardship. Even in the best favored parts of the world the human harvest includes many tares. In the most grossly overpopulated regions the amount of human wreckage is appalling.

A large part of the maldevelopment of mankind is a product of the social environment in which people spend their lives. A large part of social morals, therefore, is concerned with the creation of a kind of social order in which people are able to realize their best possibilities of development. People are not sufficiently masters of their fate and captains of their soul, to be charged with the entire responsibility for their shortcomings or their misdeeds. To a considerable extent our moral responsibilities are pooled. We are all our brothers' keepers. Even if we choose to live the life of a lone hermit in the desert, the sins of others may be due in part to the neglect of our social obligations.

Our social obligations go further, however, than the creation of favorable environmental influences. To future generations we owe in addition, the transmission of a sound heredity. That human heredity carries a burden of many defects that are a source of severe handicaps and ailments, and that it is capable of being improved in ways that would contribute greatly to the general welfare, are ideas which long remained without appreciable influence on human conduct. The desirability of perpetuating superior qualities had been recognized among the ancient Greeks (notably Theognis and Plato), but little came of this fact. Virtually nothing of note was added in this connection for over two thousand years. The scheme of human breeding set forth in Campanella's *City of the Sun* was regarded as merely the impractical dream of a fanciful philosopher, as indeed it was.

The idea of eugenic improvement was first given a sound

scientific basis by Francis Galton, whose views on this subject were suggested by reading the *Origin of Species*. The rapid advances of the science of genetics and the substantial increase of our knowledge of human heredity have clearly demonstrated the possibility of effecting marked improvements in the hereditary endowments of the human species. To have a sound physical and mental inheritance is obviously one of the greatest blessings that can fall to one's lot. It is no guarantee against falling into evil ways, but it is a precondition for the best type of development. One of the worst mishaps is to be born with a defective inheritance which may cause grave physical abnormality, imbecility, insanity, or any of the numerous other defects which result in a useless waste of life. If our race could be relieved of its inherited defects, many of the ills with which it struggles would be greatly reduced. But our aim should be higher than mere healthy mediocrity. It should be the attainment of a higher average level of physical and mental capacities. Nurture can accomplish the best results only when nature has supplied a sound foundation with which to start. Little can be accomplished with a low grade imbecile. Only those to whom nature has been generous are capable of going far.

This being true, the highest development of man obviously requires the improvement of his racial heredity. We cannot raise a fine crop of human beings without attending to both nature and nurture. The possibility of the first of these spheres of endeavor, which has only come within the purview of our moral vision within the last century, is still very imperfectly understood. In some quarters eugenics has been, and possibly still is, regarded with positive hostility. Attacks based on gross misconceptions of the subject are now less frequent than formerly, although opinions on it are still much colored by various ologies and isms.

People have been very slow to take in the fact that the

perpetuation of life includes a large part of our duties. Broadly interpreted, the proper discharge of this obligation involves not only the improvement of our biological and psychological heredity, but making the most of the offspring which are brought into the world—this by way of rounding out the process of perpetuating life and making a really good job of it. These latter functions originating in the supplementary reproductive activities, to which we have alluded in discussing the evolution of altruism, come to absorb a larger proportion of the activities of human beings, as they advance in cultural development. As a sample illustration of this fact, we may refer to the sacrifices made by parents in order to send their sons and daughters to college.

With the biological and social inheritance which he trails, both of which are fraught with many imperfections, man has evolved a series of organizations whose egoistic activities have subordinated him to their collective and frequently antagonistic interests. Dr. Reinhold Niebuhr, who looks upon man as a being fallen from grace and thereby burdened with a heavy load of original sin, almost despairs of man's ability to harmonize his group relationships. The scientific study of group behavior, with the aim of ferreting out the causes of its peculiarities, presents a relatively new field for the moral philosopher. Group behavior represents a kind of life as natural and normal as any other, in that it forms a deep-rooted phenomenon of the organic world. The basic reasons for this fact are much the same, whether it occurs in the life of a single organism or the social groups of animals or men. It is a natural outcome of the kind of selection in which the group, whether of cells or of individual organisms, acts as the unit in the struggle for existence.

True to its mode of origin, altruism typically functions in the service of some individual whole, small or large. As societies evolve and altruism becomes extended to larger and larger aggregations, subordinate organizations such as political parties, trade unions, religious bodies, etc., spring up within the wider group and sometimes threaten its disruption. The power and stability of a state require that these groups be subordinated to the interests of the whole instead of working at cross purposes. A potent factor tending to keep them in line is war, or the threat of war, and at times wars have been started for this purpose. There is no little justification for the somewhat cynical reflection that nothing stimulates friendship so much as a common enmity.

The contrast between the morality of individuals and the morality of aggregates has been forcibly brought out in Dr. Niebuhr's book on *Moral Man and Immoral Society*. Educators, social scientists, and religious idealists, according to Niebuhr, do not appreciate how ineradicably bad human societies really are. Human beings are naturally kindly, sympathetic, and adapted in many ways for living together in harmonious relations. They are surrounded by many forces which make it advantageous for them to act in conformity to the interests of their group. And it is relatively easy for the group to bring coercive measures to bear upon its members. But the behavior of groups toward one another is on a quite different basis. It is claimed by Niebuhr that moralists, as a rule, are "lacking in an understanding of the brutal character of the behavior of all human collectives, and the power of self-interest and collective egoism in all inter-group relations. Failure to recognize the stubborn resistance of group egoism to all moral and inclusive social objectives inevitably involves them in unrealistic and confused political thought. . . . It may be possible, though it is never easy, to establish just relations between individuals within a group purely by moral and religious suasion and accommodation. The relations between groups must, therefore, always be predominantly political, rather than ethical, that is, they will be determined by the proportion of power which each group possesses, at least as much as by any rational and moral appraisal of the comparative needs and claims of each group."

Either force or the threat of force is the common method by which matters of dispute have been settled when friendly negotiations fail. Dr. Niebuhr is under no illusions as to the "moral resources and limitations of human nature," and still less as to the moral resources of social groups, whether nations or organizations within nations. "The unselfishness of individuals" he tells us, "makes for the selfishness of nations. That is why the hope of solving the larger social problems of mankind, merely by extending the social sympathies of individuals, is so vain. . . . What lies beyond the nation is too vague to inspire devotion. . . . Try as he will, man seems incapable of forming an international community with power and prestige great enough to bring social restraints upon collective egoism. He has not even succeeded in disciplining anti-social group egoism within the nation. So civilization has become a device for delegating the vices of individuals to larger and larger communities. The device gives men the illusion that they are moral, but the illusion is not lasting."

To judge by his later writings, as well as by the volume referred to, Dr. Niebuhr has little faith in the ability of nations to overcome their evils ways. He does not go so far as to contend that they are inevitably foredoomed to catastrophe. He gives them a ray of hope. But I find his scheme of salvation, although the fault may be mine, somewhat lacking in precision. As a professor of Christian ethics, his general orientation on problems of human conduct is strongly influenced by certain doctrines expressed in the biblical tradition as to the relation of man to God. Among these is the doctrine of original sin. "The literal interpretation of the Fall as an historical event," he tells us, "cannot entirely obscure the profound truth which underlies the biblical conception of sin." From the standpoint of "Christianity in its profounder forms," which it may be assumed that he adopts, "man is a child of God, creature and sinner . . . his sin springs from his spiritual capacities and is defined as pride and self-glorification." Man who is finite, yet free, and "a creature who transcends the natural process to which he is related" is led through pride, as was Satan in the Miltonic epic, to insubordination and revolt. Man, as I gather from Niebuhr's discussion, may find it impossible to redeem himself through his own efforts, and may have to rely upon the prophecy of Jesus that "the triumph would have to come through the intervention of God," because "the moral resources of man would not be sufficient to guarantee it."

It must be admitted that there is much basis for Dr. Niebuhr's rather gloomy outlook. While the Second World War removed some immediate dangers to civilization, the wrangling that has followed it has emphasized his conception of the essentially egoistic nature of national groups. The world faces problems resulting from group egoism which now seem more serious than ever before. I cannot share Dr. Niebuhr's views as to the source of the sinful state of man, which I am convinced are too much influenced by supernaturalism to be helpful. Group egoism is an inevitable product of the forces which have made us social. In popular parlance, we came by it honestly. Perhaps this fact may render group egoism more amenable to control in the interests of the general weal. Or, again, it may prove to be incapable of control and plunge the world into chaos. Having no gift of prophecy, I cannot decide between these alternatives. The peoples of the world face their testing time with very inadequate preparation for dealing with the great issues which have been thrust into prominence by the logic of events.

In the fields of physical science man has accomplished truly wonderful things. He is there dealing with material he can rely upon. When he is concerned with his own kind, his endeavor to attain a scientific understanding of his subject matter appears to have made relatively slow progress. Yet, when we compare our present knowledge of man's nature with that prevailing during the Renaissance, or even in the eighteenth century, we must recognize many advances which have been of great service in connection with problems of human relations. That groups should be predominantly self-centered and antagonistic is a natural consequence of the reasons for their development. The struggle for existence has often led nations to unite for purposes of defense, temporarily as in the two world wars, or permanently as in the formation of the German empire. The permanent unions have largely eliminated the hostilities of their component parts. Trade relations to the advantage of all parties concerned, together with travel and the exchange of ideas, have been unifying forces tending to promote better understanding and good feeling between different peoples. Optimists formerly looked upon these forces as fraught with promise of an era of international friendship and harmony. But while these forces continue to work toward this end, the extension of economic interests beyond national borders, and especially into relatively backward and undeveloped countries, tends to breed antagonisms that endanger peace.

One notorious source of international discord is economic imperialism. The case is stated by J. A. Hobson as follows:

"If the struggle of rival imperialisms and their economic policies continues, no serious hopes or expectations of lasting world peace can be entertained, for all the seeds of strife remain in the world system. On the economic side, the international struggles for raw resources such as oil, rubber, copper, the deficiency of foreign markets adequate to take the export surpluses which depressed trades in industrial countries could produce, the visible waste of manufacturing power thus revealed, the raising of tariff walls and other aids to home industries at the expense of foreigners, the payment of war debts by poorer nations to richer, the harassing fluctuations of foreign exchange—all these factors feed international fears, suspicions, envies, and hatreds. The only escape from these moral and economic wastes and perils is by way of organized economic internationalism."

Any kind of organization which may be set up to settle international disputes will encounter great difficulties so long as unregulated economic rivalries are continually sowing the seeds of strife. The attainment of secure and lasting peace requires so many reforms that must inevitably come slowly, that perhaps the most that can be hoped from such an organization is that it may tide us over an acutely dangerous period until some of these changes can be effected. At present there is little to indicate that in the near future any effective cooperative efforts will be made to prevent economic rivalries from continuing to menace the peace of the world.

APPENDIX

Bibliographical References and Comments

FOR THE BENEFIT of those readers who desire to pursue further some of the topics briefly discussed in the preceding pages, I have added a number of references which I hope may prove useful. Since so many kinds of activity have a moral import in one way or another, a great deal of the literature that is most significant for the scientific student of morals, whose investigations often lead him into strange territory, is to be found under other headings. The attempt to cover the whole field would of course involve an endless task. A good general bibliography on ethics is included in the third volume, part 2, of J. M. Baldwin's *Dictionary of Philosophy and Psychology* (N.Y., 1905). There is a briefer but more recent bibliography in C. L. Barrett's *Ethics* (N.Y., 1933); and H. L. Mencken's *Treatise on Right and Wrong* (N.Y., 1934) has a useful final section of bibliographical notes. The bibliography of Westermarck's monumental *Origin and Development of the Moral Ideas* is especially useful for its numerous references to anthropological, historical, philosophical and religious literature. The same remark applies to a less degree to the references in Spencer's *Principles of Ethics* and *Principles of Sociology*. Current references are compiled in the annual volumes of *The Psychological Index*.

Ethics is the most important journal devoted exclusively to the field. See also *The Standard* issued by the American Ethical Union, N.Y. Other current literature is widely scattered in journals dealing with philosophy, psychology, religion, the social sciences, and in the more popular magazines. Hastings's *Encyclopaedia of Religion and Ethics* (N.Y., 1908–1927) is a valuable general reference, as is the *Catholic Encyclopaedia* for Catholic viewpoints. Two useful compilations of the writings of the representatives of different schools are B. Rand's *The Classical Moralists* (Boston, 1909), and Selby-Bigge's *British Moralists* (2 vols., Oxford, 1897).

From the nature of the subject a great many books on ethics deal with various phases of its history. The student may consult with profit the larger histories of philosophy by Ueberweg, Erdmann, and especially Windelband (rev. ed., N.Y., 1921). H. Sidgwick's *History of Ethics* (6th ed., N.Y., 1901) covers the field in a judicious and scholarly manner. Lecky's well-known *History of European Morals* deals with the period from Augustus to Charlemagne. Much valuable material is contained also in the *History of Rationalism in Europe* by the same writer. The second volume of Wundt's *Ethics* (3 vols., London, 1897-1901) is devoted to a historical exposition of various systems from early to recent times. E. S. Wake's *The Evolution of Morality* (2 vols., London, 1878) is concerned largely with the moral customs of different peoples. A. K. Rogers's *Morals in Review* (N.Y., 1927) discusses various systems from the Greeks to the present. *The Evolution of Ethics* edited by E. H. Sneath (Yale University Press, 1927) contains discussions by various specialists on the ethics of the Greeks, Hindus, Egyptians, Hebrews, Persians, Romans and other peoples of the ancient world. Most valuable of all the general histories is Jodl's monumental *Geschichte der Ethik* (Stuttgart, 1926), which treats of the development of the subject, with true Teutonic thoroughness, from the earliest to recent times. All students of the history of ethics will be grateful for R. A. Tsanoff's recent survey of *The Moral Ideas of Our Civilization* (N.Y., 1942).

Of the multitude of books dealing with the ethics of Christianity I shall call attention only to H. H. Henson's *Christian Morality* (Oxford, 1936), D. S. Adam's *A Handbook of Christian Ethics* (Edinburgh, 1935), and Westermarck's *Christianity and Morals* (N.Y., 1939). The latter book is quite unusual in treating the subject objectively from the standpoint of the student of the natural history of morals. It is thoroughly documented and gives the authorities for its numerous statements of facts, and hence affords a valuable guide to one who wishes to explore further in this field.

In the modern period, one of the most disturbing contributions to ethical theory was expounded in *Leviathan* by Thomas Hobbes which is now issued in one of the volumes of Everyman's Library. The ethical heresies of Hobbes, which it was held must on no account be left unchallenged, elicited replies from Cudworth, Cumberland, Locke, Clarke, Hutcheson, Bishop Butler, H. More and Shaftesbury, all of whom developed moral philosophies of their own. In this connection one should mention B. Mandeville's *Fable of the Bees, or Private Vices, Public Benefits,* in which the author scandalized the good people of his day by making a cynical plea for the social value of pure egoism. The idea suggests the viewpoint developed later, but in more acceptable phraseology, in the celebrated work of Adam Smith on *The Wealth of Nations* and in the writings of subsequent *laissez faire* economists. Hedonism, which seems to be an inevitable product of free speculative thought, passed out of its purely egoistic stage in the hands of the more influential moralists. The chief development in this line occurred in Great Britain, and an account of the writings of its chief leaders is given in Albee's *A History of English Utilitarianism* (N.Y., 1902) and in Leslie Stephen's *The English Utilitarians* (2 vols., London, 1900). Bentham's principal writings on morals are contained in his *Deontology* (2 vols., London and Edinburgh, 1834) and *An Introduction to the Principles of Morals and Legislation* (Oxford, 1879). J. S. Mill has discussed ethical problems in a number of books, but his chief contribution is his well-known essay on *Utilitarianism* (London, 1863). After Mill, about the ablest defense of utilitarianism is made in Sidgwick's *Methods of Ethics* (rev. ed., N.Y., 1901). The following two important works are essentially utilitarian, although they preceded the more explicit development of that doctrine in the hands of Bentham: David Hume, *An Inquiry Concerning the Principles of Morals,* 1751, and Adam Smith's *The Theory of Moral Sentiments,* 1759. For a more accessible discussion of Hume see T. H. Huxley's *Hume* (London, 1879).

Passing to the intuitionists, whom it is often difficult to classify, even to the extent of deciding whether they should be called intuitionists or not, we may cite the following as fairly representative of this school; R. Price, *Review of the Principal Questions in Morals* (London, 1757); Thomas Reid, *Essays on the Intellectual Powers of Man,* 1788; D. Stewart, *The Philosophy of the Active and Moral Powers* (2 vols., Edinburgh, 1828); Thomas Brown, *Lectures on the Philosophy of the Human Mind,* 1820; William Whewell, *Elements of Morality* (Cambridge, 1864); F. P. Cobbe, *The Theory of Intuitive Morals,* 1855; J. Martineau, *Types of Ethical Theory* (2 vols., Oxford, 1885).

Kant's two chief treatises on ethics are *The Fundamental Principles of the Metaphysics of Morals,* and the *Critique of the Practical Reason* both of which have been translated by T. K. Abbot under the title Kant's *Theory of Ethics* (6th ed., London, 1923). See also J. W. Scott, *Kant on the Moral Life* (N.Y., 1924). Of the many expositions and criticisms of Kant's ethics, J. G. Schurman's *Kantian Ethics and the Ethics of Evolution* (London, 1881) is of especial relevance to the subject matter of the present volume.

Ethical thought in Germany was profoundly affected by the development of post-Kantian idealistic philosophy in the hands of Fichte, Schelling, Hegel and (in a quite different way) Schopenhauer, and this influence later became very potent in other countries. Especially noteworthy products of this movement in its early period are Fichte's *The Science of Ethics* (translation by Kroeger, London, 1897) and Hegel's *Philosophy of Right* (translation by Dyde, 1896). The impress of Hegelianism on ethical thought in England is very marked, as may be exemplified by two able and influential books, T. H. Green's *Prolegomena to Ethics* (Oxford, 1883) and F. H. Bradley's *Ethical Studies* (London, 1876; 2nd ed., Oxford, 1927).

Of the more or less didactic works intended for use as textbooks or designed to give the reader a general orientation in the subject, I can mention only a small proportion. In many of these books the authors, in addition to expounding subject matter, have an axe of their own to grind in setting forth their own peculiar standpoint and in showing where other ethicists have gone wrong. Utilitarianism usually comes in for a drubbing, but on the constructive side one finds a variety of standpoints. The short list selected contains only books by writers of acknowledged competence in their fields. Among the very best expositions, characterized both by penetrating insight and sound common sense, is Dewey and Tufts' *Ethics* (N.Y., 1910). Among other good expositions are Mackenzie, *A Manual of Ethics* (6th ed., London, 1929); J. Seth, *A Study of Ethical Principles* (11th ed., N.Y., 1910); W. Fite, *An Introduction to the Study of Ethics* (N.Y., 1909) and *Moral Philosophy* (N.Y., 1925); J. H. Muirhead, *The Elements of Ethics* (4th ed., London, 1932); T. De Laguna, *Introduction to the Science of Ethics* (N.Y., 1914); F. C. Sharp, *Ethics* (N.Y., 1928); F. Paulsen, *System of Ethics* (N.Y., 1908); W. M. Urban, *Fundamentals of Ethics* (N.Y., 1930); C. L. Barrett, *Ethics* (N.Y., 1933). A. Bain's *Moral Science* is still useful, though no longer modern.

Among the expository and critical books of more comprehensive scope than most of the preceding texts, I may cite: James Martineau, *Types of Ethical Theory* (2 vols., Oxford, 1885); William Wundt, *Ethics* (3 vols., London, 1897-1901); the valuable comprehensive work of H. Rashdall on *The Theory of Good and Evil* (2 vols., Oxford, 1924); A. E. Taylor, *The Problem of Conduct* (London, 1900); G. Simmel's unfortunately untranslated *Einleitung in die Moralwissenschaft* (2 vols., Berlin, 1892-1893), in which the author arrives at views on the standard of morals quite opposed to those of most moralists; N. Hartmann's *Ethics*, translated by S. Coit, (3 vols., London, 1932); H. Sidgwick, *The Methods of Ethics* (7th ed., London, 1922), a work of deservedly high repute. S. E. Mezes, *Ethics* (N.Y., 1901) contains a full discussion of conscience from the naturalistic standpoint. See also the able volume of T. V. Smith, *Beyond Conscience* (N.Y., 1934). Several of the essays in the noteworthy volume on *Naturalism and the Human Spirit* (edited by Krikorian, N.Y., 1945) treat of ethics from the naturalistic standpoint.

Evolutionary ethics is discussed with various attitudes of approval, condescension and hostility in a large number of volumes, but I must limit myself to books devoted largely to this topic. A very useful survey for its time is given in Cora M. Williams's *A Review of the Systems of Ethics Founded on the Theory of Evolution* (N.Y., 1893). The earlier views of Spencer, which, despite his criticisms of Bentham and Mill, were essentially utilitarian, were embodied in his *Social Statics,* which appeared in 1850. The application of the theory of evolution to ethics which had been made, to a certain extent, in his *Principles of Psychology* in 1855 and in some of his essays (viz., *Morals and Moral Sentiments,* 1871), became the keynote to Spencer's two bulky volumes on *The Principles of Ethics* (1879-1893). In addition to the many concrete facts included in the *Principles of Ethics,* there is a great wealth of data bearing on moral problems in the three volumes of his *Principles of Sociology* (London, 1879-1896) and in the eight volumes of his *Descriptive Sociology* (London, 1873-1881).

The contributions of Darwin are embodied in *The Descent of Man* (London, 1871) and in *The Expression of the Emotions in Man and Animals* (London, 1872). One of the earliest books in which the operation of group selection is emphasized in the evolution of morals is W. Bagehot's able volume on *Physics and Politics* (London, 1873). The striking essays that marked the intrepid incursions of W. K. Clifford into the field of ethics made their first appearance in different periodicals, 1875 to 1877, but they were subsequently issued in the second volume of Clifford's *Lectures and Essays* edited by Leslie Stephen and Frederick Pollock (London, 1879). Leslie Stephen's *The Science of Ethics* (London, 1882) ranks among the ablest expositions from the evolutionary point of view. Where he differs from Spencer he makes out a very good case. Professor S. Alexander's *Moral Order and Progress* (London, 1891) is an able and scholarly treatment of evolutionary ethics from the philosophical standpoint.

A. Sutherland's large two-volume treatise on *The Origin and Growth of the Moral Instinct* (London, 1898) is a veritable mine of information on the parental and social behavior of animals and savage and barbaric human beings. E. Westermarck's monumental *Origin and Development of the Moral Ideas*. I cannot praise too highly for its vast assemblage of facts concerning the life of many races and peoples both past and present. It is an absolutely indispensable work for all inductive students of the moral life. In a later volume on *Ethical Relativity* (N.Y., 1933) the author sets forth his general standpoint on moral problems much as he has done in the earlier chapters of the previous work, and he reinforces his conclusions by his habitually copious array of facts and references. Another valuable work more or less similar in kind to Westermarck's *Treatise* is L. T. Hobhouse's *Morals in Evolution* (London, 1904, 4th ed., 1923). The author has expounded his general philosophy of morals in *The Rational Good* (N.Y., 1921).

Among the writings of Nietzsche, who has figured spectacularly as the bad boy among modern moralists, I may cite *The Genealogy of Morals, Beyond Good and Evil,* and *Thus Spake Zarathustra,* as containing the author's most important declamatory expositions of his views. As a sort of counteractive of Nietzsche's extolment of ruthless strife I may refer to two books by P. Kropotkin, *Mutual Aid as a Factor in Evolution* (London, 1902) and his posthumously published *Ethics* (London, 1924). Bearing also on the ethical import of the struggle for existence is T. H. Huxley's celebrated Romanes lecture on *Evolution and Ethics* (London, 1893). In the same connection may be cited two books by A. Machin, *The Ascent of Man by Means of Natural Selection* (London, 1925) and *Darwin's Theory Applied to Mankind* (London, 1937).

A very good small volume, unfortunately too little known, on what I may venture to call Darwinian ethics applied to everyday life, is E. B. Copeland's *Natural Conduct* (Stanford University Press, 1928). Professor W. E. Ritter's and E. W. Bailey's book, *The Natural History of Our Conduct* (N.Y., 1927), shows how animals and human beings behave in many ways that are very much alike, both in their adaptive and their maladaptive activities. The bibliography is concerned chiefly with the moral and the immoral behavior of mammals, birds, reptiles and insects. And this reminds me of a little book by L. Bauke, who writes under the pseudonym of T. Zell, on *Moral in der Tierwelt* (Leipzig, 1920).

Of the books making extensive appeal to the doctrine of evolution in the interpretation of human nature and human behavior, there are now to be included many treatises on psychology. Among these a position of especial prominence is to be given to the classical work of William James on *The Principles of Psychology* (2 vols., N.Y., 1890), and E. L. Thorndike's *Educational Psychology* (3 vols., N.Y., 1912-1914). See also Thorndike's *Human Nature and the Social Order* (N.Y., 1940), and J. G. Needham's recent volume, *About Ourselves* (Lancaster, Pa., 1941). G. Stanley Hall's two bulky volumes on *Adolescence* deserve also a prominent place in this connection. Many valuable original ideas are to be found in J. M. Baldwin's two volumes, *Social and Ethical Interpretations* (3rd ed., N.Y., 1906), and *Mental Development in the Child and in the Race* (2nd ed., N.Y., 1903). Much help in understanding human beings is to be derived also from C. Cooley's *Human Nature and the Social Order* (rev. ed., N.Y., 1922). See also D. Irons, *A Study in the Psychology of Ethics* (London, 1903), and also William McDougall, *Social Psychology* (Boston, 1926), whose favorable reception, despite considerable criticism of its instinct psychology, is attested by its having passed through twenty editions. Of late years there has been a flood of books on social psychology of varying degrees of merit, but I shall not attempt to appraise them.

A list of books on the evolutionary interpretation of human behavior would not be complete that did not include a few references on the psychology of the pithecoid relatives of man. Among recent studies may be mentioned R. M. Yerkes's *Almost Human* (N.Y., 1925); and R. M. Yerkes's and A. W. Yerkes's *The Great Apes* (N.Y., 1929). See also S. Zuckermann, *The Social Life of Monkeys and Apes* (London, 1932). An unusually illuminating treatise on human nature is W. Köhler's *The Mentality of Apes* (N.Y., 1925), especially the parts dealing with emotional life.

J. G. Schurman's *Ethical Import of Darwinianism,* which has been discussed briefly in preceding pages, is one of the ablest criticisms of Darwin's ethical views. Reference should be made also to W. R. Sorley, *On the Ethics of Naturalism* (Edinburgh and London, 1885), and J. T. Bixby, *The Crisis in Morals* (Boston, 1891).

The following books on morals may be commended on various grounds, among others the fact that they get out of the traditional ruts: J. Dewey, *Human Nature and Conduct* (N.Y., 1922), and his recent *Problems of Men* (N.Y., 1946); W. Lippmann, *A Preface to Morals* (N.Y., 1931), a readable volume written from a nonmetaphysical and naturalistic standpoint and dealing with several current moral problems. H. L. Mencken, *A Treatise on Right and Wrong* (N.Y., 1934), also quite unmetaphysical and critical of ecclesiastical ethics of all sorts. One might dip into it at random and soon be sure that it was written by H. L. Mencken. It is a kind of companion volume to the author's *Treatise on the Gods,* but better. D. Drake, *The New Morality* (N.Y., 1928) and *Problems of Conduct* (2nd ed., N.Y., 1935) both contain vigorous and independent treatments of current moral problems. William McDougall's *Ethics and Some Modern World Problems* (N.Y., 1924) contrasts national systems of ethics, such as the Hebrew, with international systems, such as Christianity and Buddhism, with evaluations of their respective merits and drawbacks.

Concerning the moral customs of savage and barbaric peoples, the best reference is Westermarck's *History of Moral Ideas* with its extensive bibliography. Much material is contained in E. B. Tylor's *Primitive Culture* (2 vols., London, 1874), in Spencer's writings on sociology and ethics, and in Sutherland. W. G. Sumner's *Folkways* is very valuable. Other useful references are A. L. Kroeber, *Anthropology* (N.Y., 1923); A. A. Goldenweiser, *Early Civilization* (N.Y., 1922); R. H. Lowie, *Are We Civilized?* (N.Y., 1929); C. Wissler, *Man and Culture* (N.Y., 1923); and L. T. Hobhouse, *Morals in Evolution.* On marriage customs in primitive society see Westermarck's *History of Human Marriage* (3rd ed., N.Y., 1902); Spencer, *Principles of Sociology;* G. E. Howard, *A History of Matrimonial Institutions* (Chicago, 1904); R. Briffault, *The Mothers* (London, 1927); B. Malinowski, *Sex and Repression in Savage Society* (N.Y., 1927), and Westermarck's recent volume on *The Future of Marriage in Western Civilization*

(N.Y., 1936) which, although dealing chiefly with modern conditions, makes frequent comparisons with primitive customs.

Besides the discussions on the relation of religion to the evolution of morals in the works of Tylor, Spencer, Wundt, Lecky, Sumner, Westermarck and Hobhouse referred to elsewhere, I may add J. G. Frazer, *The Golden Bough,* which has now grown to colossal proportions (3rd ed., 12 vols., London, 1911-1915); Conybeare, *Myth, Magic and Morals* (London, 1909); R. H. Lowie, *Primitive Religion* (N.Y., 1924); L. Lévy-Bruhl, *Primitive Mentality* (N.Y., 1923); R. R. Marett, *The Threshold of Religion* (N.Y., 1909); B. Kidd, *Social Evolution* (London, 1894) and the *Principles of Western Civilization* (London, 1902). On the psychology of religion see E. D. Starbuck, *The Psychology of Religion* (N.Y., 1899), based largely on inductive research; William James, *The Varieties of Religious Experience* (London, 1902), and J. B. Pratt, *The Psychology of Religious Belief* (N.Y., 1907).

The following references relate to the topics discussed in chapter 10: W. F. Wilcox, *The Divorce Problem* (N.Y., 1891); J. P. Lichtenberger, *Divorce* (N.Y., 1931); B. B. Lindsay and W. Evans, *The Revolt of Modern Youth* (N.Y., 1928) and *The Companionate Marriage* (N.Y., 1928); V. F. Calverton, *The Bankruptcy of Marriage* (London, 1931); A. Cohen, *Statistical Analysis of American Marriage* (N.Y., 1932); E. R. Maurer, *Family Disorganization* (Chicago, 1939); B. Russell *et al., Divorce* (N.Y., 1930) presents different viewpoints of several contributors; chapter 10 on Divorce in Westermarck's *The Future of Marriage in Western Civilization* gives an account of the present divorce situation in different countries with many references.

On birth control there is now a multitude of books, among which those of Margaret Sanger deserve especial mention. A partial list of these includes *The Pivot of Civilization* (N.Y., 1922), *The New Motherhood* (London, 1922) and *Motherhood in Bondage* (N.Y., 1928). A few other references are M. Stopes, *Contraception* (London, 1923); W. H. Smith, *Children by Chance or by Choice* (Boston, 1920); N. E. Himes, *The Truth about Birth Control* (N.Y., 1931); F. W. White, *Birth Control and Its Opponents* (London, 1935). Attacks upon birth control are to be found in J. M. Cooper, *Birth Control* (Washington, 1923); H. G. Sutherland, *Birth Control* (N.Y., 1922), *Control of Life* (London, 1944); and E. R. Moore, *The Case Against Birth Control* (N.Y., 1931). The two principal journals are *Human Fertility* (Baltimore) and *The New Generation* (London). A fairly comprehensive bibliography on birth control up to 1924 will be found in my *Bibliography of Eugenics* (University of California Press, 1924), pp. 341–354.

As to the vivisection question, a large part of the literature on the striking advances of medical science, such as De Kruif's *Microbe Hunters,* to take but a single example, might be cited as yielding evidence justifying experimentation on living animals. Of the books devoted explicitly to arguing the pros and cons of the question I shall limit myself to three that present different viewpoints; W. W. Keen, *Animal Experimentation and Medical Progress* (Boston, 1914); A. Leffingwell, *An Ethical Problem* (London, 1914); and S. Paget, *For and Against Experiments on Animals* (N.Y., 1912).

Most of the books dealing with the racial effects of war are inspired by the aim of proving that war is bad, biologically, culturally, and in every other way. They may be largely right, but they generally give an oversimplified solution of a very complex problem. This is true of the well known books of D. S. Jordan on *The Blood of the Nation, The Human Harvest,* and *War and the Breed,* P. C. Mitchell's *Evolution and the War* and Norman Angell's *The Great Illusion* (London, 1910; rev. ed., 1939). A variant from the usual standpoint is presented in J. F. Carter's *Man Is War* (Indianapolis, 1926). General Bernhardi's *Germany and the Next War* (N.Y., 1914) apparently represented the later dominant war philosophy of his country. The most thoroughgoing and adequate analysis of the varied effects of war is S. R. Steinmetz's *Die Soziologie des Krieges* (Leipzig, 1929), which is a revised and greatly augmented edition of the author's *Philosophie des Krieges* (Leipzig, 1907). Other useful books are G. F. Nicolai, *The Biology of War* (N.Y., 1918); G. W. Nasmyth, *Social Progress and the Darwinian Theory* (N.Y., 1916); J. A. Novicow, *War and Its Alleged Benefits* (N.Y., 1911); W. Trotter, *Instincts of the Herd in Peace and War* (N.Y., 1916); F. Prinzing,

Epidemics Resulting from Wars (Oxford, 1916); and G. Bodart and V. L. Kellogg, *Losses of Life in Modern Wars* (Oxford, 1916); and Q. Wright, *A Study of War* (Chicago, 1942). H. K. Norton's *Back of War* (N.Y., 1928) contains a valuable, scholarly and balanced treatment of the various causes that incite peoples to conflict. It deserves a high rating among the books in its field. M. R. Davie's *The Evolution of War; A Study of its Rôle in Early Societies* (New Haven, 1929) is a valuable contribution and contains a full bibliography. E. F. M. Durbin and J. Bowlby have made a noteworthy study of one phase of the problem in their small volume on *Personal Aggression and War* in which they contend that a prime cause of war is the natural aggressiveness of the human animal, and they support their position by adducing much concrete evidence from the behavior of animals, children, and the adults of both primitive and civilized peoples. On the subject of pugnacity in general I may refer to P. Bovet, *The Fighting Instinct* (London, 1923), and G. M. Stratton, *Anger* (N.Y., 1922).

Especial emphasis on the causes of war and the problem of its prevention is laid in L. L. Bernard's *War and Its Causes* (N.Y., 1944), and the essays edited by G. Murphy on *Human Nature and Enduring Peace* (Boston, 1945). Much illuminating material on the forces that make for war is presented in F. L. Schuman's bulky volume on *International Politics* (N.Y., 1933).

On the ethics of forming opinions the reader may be interested in the position taken by William James in *The Will to Believe* (N.Y., 1897) and also in the attitude of Cardinal Newman as stated in *An Essay in Aid of a Grammar of Assent* (London, 1870). Then, if the shock of transition does not prove too much for him, he might try H. Ward's breezy volume entitled *Thobbing* (Indianapolis, 1926), which inveighs against wishful thinking in all fields. There is some very wholesome gospel on the subject in A. E. Wiggam's stimulating volume on *The Marks of an Educated Man* (N.Y., 1930). Clifford's essays on *The Ethics of Belief* and *The Ethics of Religion,* which were quoted in a previous chapter, appear in the second volume of his *Lectures and Essays* (London, 1879).

Index

Abbot, T. K., 217
Abd-el-Lateef, 168
Adam, D. S., 215
Adams, G. P., ix
Affection, 65, 67, 93–95
Agoraphobia, 78
Ahriman, 72
Albee, E., 216
Alexander, S., 55, 219
Altruism, 91, 92, 95, 99, 102–115
Ambrose, Saint, 191
American Indians, 97, 119, 120, 123, 126, 128
Angell, N., 201, 224
Anger, 65, 74, 75, 79–84, 91
Anglo-Saxons, 54, 198
Animism, 130–133
Antivivisection, 162–165
Aquinas, Thomas, 21, 139
Aristippus, 44
Aristotle, 20, 26, 45, 104
Association psychology, 57, 58, 103
Augustine, Saint, 149, 191
Austin, J., 46
Authoritarian ethics, 17–22, 145–162, 167–174

Bacon, F., 73
Bagehot, W., 128, 219
Bailey, E. W., 220
Bain, A., 62, 93, 94, 103, 218
Baldwin, J. M., 55, 86, 87, 214, 221
Balfour, A. J., 9
Barnes, H. E., 205
Barrett, C. L., 214, 218
Bashfulness, 86–89
Bauke, L., 220
Bees, 107
Behaviorism, 1

Belief, ethics of, 165–175
Benn, A. W., 7
Bentham, J., 22–25, 44, 46, 57, 216, 219
Berkeley, G., 73
Bernard, L. L., 225
Bernhardi, Gen. F. A. J., 224
Bible, ethics of, 45
Birth control, 153–159
Bixby, J. T., 222
Blushing, 87–89
Bock, C., 123
Bodart, G., 225
Bovet, P., 225
Bowlby, J., 225
Bradley, F. H., 31, 33, 34, 217
Brahmans, 49, 178
Bridgewater Treatises, 8
Briffault, R., 222
Brooke, J., 122, 123
Brown, T., 27, 28, 217
Browne, T., 167 note
Buddhists, 178
Burke, E., 202
Butler, Bishop J., 27, 56, 216

Caird, E., 31–33
Calverton, V. F., 223
Calvinism, 49, 143
Campanella, T., 206
Cannon, W., 74
Carter, J. F., 224
Categorical imperative, 29–34, 45, 64
Catholic Church, ethical teaching, 74, 148–151, 170, 173
Cells, behavior of, 1–4
Chimpanzees, 80, 92, 114, 121
Chipewyans, 51, 123
Chesterton, G. K., on euthanasia, 161

227

INDEX

Christianity, ethics of, 20–22, 72, 145–158, 167–169, 172, 173, 210, 211
Clarke, S., 216
Class war, 188
Clifford, W. K., 68, 165, 166, 174
Cobbe, F. P., 217
Cohen, A., 223
Coit, S., 218
Communism, 182, 183
Communist Manifesto, 182
Comte, A., vi
Conscience, 27–29, 52, 56–70, 90, 136
Conybeare, F. C., 223
Cooley, C., 82, 221
Cooper, J. M., 155, 224
Copeland, E. B., 220
Cowper, W., 191
Crime, 96, 97, 127, 204, 205
Cudworth, R., 216
Cumberland, R., 216

Darwin, C. R., 6, 35–37, 39, 41, 49–52, 59–68, 73–75, 80, 88, 89, 112, 197, 219
Darwinian theory, 3, 35, 39–41, 43, 48, 71, 74, 95, 96, 103, 198
Davie, M. R., 225
De Kruif, P., 224
De Laguna, T., 218
Demoniacal possession, 13
Descartes, R., 73
Descent of Man, The, 6, 60–65, 197, 219
Design argument, 8, 10
Development, 2–4
Dewey, J., viii, 5, 16, 31, 218, 222
Dickens, C., 25
Dieri, treachery of, 123
Dielanger, 123
Differentiation, 3
Divorce, 148–153
Dorman, R. M., on N. Am. Indians, 120
Drake, D., 222
Dryden, J., on pride, 90
Dueling, 80, 86, 176, 177
Durbin, E. F. M., 225
Duty, 30–32, 64

Dyaks, of Borneo, 81, 122, 123
Dyde, S. W., 217

Economic rivalry, 188, 189, 212, 213
Egoism, 66, 96–99, 102–104, 189
Eliot, George, 202
Elliot, W., 123
Ellis, H., 11 note
Emerson, R. W., 71
Erdmann, J. E., 215
Eskimos, 126, 134
Ethical Relativity, 41, 220
Eugenics, 206–208
Euthanasia, 159–162
Evans, W., 223

Fabre, J. H., 105
Fear, 65, 75–79, 87, 91, 133, 135
Fichte, J., 217
Fijians, 119
Fish, care of eggs, 107
Fite, W., 218
Frazer, J. G., 223
Frederick the Great, on war, 194

Galileo, 151
Galton, F., 113, 207
Gason, S., 123
Genes, 3
Gifford Lectures, 8, 9
Godwin, W., 44
Goldenweiser, A. A., 222
Gorillas, 77, 110
Greeks, ethical speculations, vii, 16, 20, 21
Green, T. H., 31, 33, 69, 217
Greenlanders, honesty, 123
Grey, Sir George, 125
Grotius, H., 193
Group morality, 208–213
Group selection, 81, 111–114, 198–201, 208

Hall, G. S., 83, 97, 221
Happiness, 21–23, 25–27, 35–38, 40, 47
Hartley, D., 73, 103
Hartmann, R., on family life among gorillas, 110

INDEX

Hartmann, N., 218
Hastings, J., 214
Hayes, Cardinal P. J., 155, 156
Hebrews, ethics of, 18, 19
Hedonism, 21, 38, 40, 102
Hegel, G. W. F., 31, 33, 45, 217
Helvetius, C. A., 24, 44
Henson, H. H., 215
Heretics, persecution of, 57, 139, 140
Himes, N. E., 223
Hippocrates, viii
Hitler, A., 181, 196
Hobbes, T., 21, 24, 44, 73, 125, 216
Hobhouse, L. T., 100, 116, 120, 220, 222, 223
Hobson, E. W., 10
Hobson, J. A., 185, 186, 212
D'Holbach, 24
Holmes, J. H., 193, 194
Holmes, S. J., 224
Homicide, 118, 126
Hottentots, 119, 128
Howard, G. E., 222
Howard, J., 115
Hudson, W. H., 76
Human selection, 53
Hume, D., 22, 73, 144, 216
Humiliation, 65
Hutcheson, F., 22, 216
Huxley, T. H., 216, 220

Igorrotes, 51
Infanticide, 118
Inge, Dean, on euthanasia, 159
Instinct, 28, 39, 50–52, 60–63, 98, 111
Intuitionism, 27, 28, 45, 48
Irons, D., 221
Israel, Children of, 18, 19, 124

Jacobi, W., on Kantian ethics, 32
James, W., 11, 23, 98, 174, 221, 223, 225
Jealousy, 78, 83, 84
Jehovah, 18–20, 136
Jesus, 20, 25, 148, 149, 193, 211
Jews, 18–20
Jodl, F., 215
Jordan, D. S., 200, 224

Kafirs, 126
Kant, I., 29–32, 34, 45, 48 56, 65, 66, 145, 217
Keen, W. W., 224
Kellogg, V. L., 225
Kidd, B., 223
Kingsford, Anne, 164
Knox, J., 143
Köhler, W., 92, 114, 121, 221
Kolben, P., 119
Krikorian, Y. H., 218
Kroeber, A. L., 222
Kroeger, A. E., 217
Kropotkin, P., 220
Ku Klux Klan, 188
Kurubars, 123

Lamarck, J. B., 73
Lamarckism, 59, 60, 73, 88
de La Rochefoucauld, F., 84
Leake, C., ix
Lecky, W. E. H., 27, 57, 100, 138, 149, 215, 223
Leffingwell, A., 224
Lévy-Bruhl, L., 223
Lex talionis, 127, 148, 204
Lichtenberger, J. P., 223
Lindsay, B. B., 223
Line-af-Hagely, Miss, 164
Lippmann, W., 222
Locke, J., 73, 216
Love, 62, 93, 95
Love, J. R. B., 126
Lowie, R. H., ix, 117, 222, 223
Lubbock, Sir J., 120
Luther, M., 102, 138

Macaulay, T. B., 26
Machin, A., 53, 220
Mackenzie, J. S., 218
Maladaptiveness, 137–141
Malinowski, B., 222
Mandeville, B., 24, 44, 216
Marett, R. R., 223
Martineau, J., 217, 218
Marx, K., 182
Masai, honesty, 124
Maurer, E. R., 223
McDougall, W., 81, 93, 221, 222

INDEX

McTaggart, J. M. E., 33
Mencken, H. L., 214, 222
Mezes, S. E., 218
Mill, J. S., 23–25, 44, 46, 47, 57, 103, 216, 219
Mitchell, P. C., 224
Modesty, 86–88
Mohammedanism, 54, 143
Moore, E. R., 156, 224
Moral sense, 27–29, 52, 56–70, 90
More, H., 216
Morgan, L. H., 118
Moses, 18, 124
Muirhead, J. H., 27, 33, 218
Murphy, G., 225
Mutation, 3
Mystics, 174

Nasmyth, G. W., 224
Natural selection, 3, 35, 36, 39, 40, 50–55, 60, 61, 66, 71, 113, 197–201
Natural theology, 8, 10, 11, 22
Naturalism, 5, 7, 9, 11, 12, 15, 48
Needham, J. G., 221
Nelson, E. W., 126
Nevill, H., 123
Newman, J. H., 173, 225
New Zealanders, 131,
Nicolai, G. F., 224
Niebuhr, R., 208–211
Nietzsche, F. W., 220
Nightingale, F., 115
Norton, H. K., 225
Novicow, J. A., 224

Old Testament, ethics of, 18, 19, 124, 136
Origin of Species, 6, 207
Ormuzd, 72
Osmia papaveris, 105, 107

Pacifism, 191–194
Paget, S., 224
Pain, 21–24, 32, 36
Paley, W., 8, 10, 21, 22, 45
Palgrave, W. G., 168
Parental care, 107–110
Paulsen, F., 45, 218
Pepper, S. C., ix

Perry, R. B., 1
Pfeiffer, Ida, 123
Pius XI, Pope, 149, 150, 154, 158
Plato, 20, 45, 206
Pleasure, 21–27, 32, 36, 40, 43, 44, 47, 60–62
Pollock, F., 219
Pratt, J. B., 223
Price, R., 27, 45, 217
Priestly, J., 44, 46
Prinzing, F., 224, 225
Prophets, 19, 136
Proverbs, 19
Psalms, 19, 136
Pugnacity, 79–83, 111, 112, 121, 122
Puritans, 26

Quillian, W. S., 11

Radin, P., 133
Rand, B., 215
Rashdall, H., 31, 34, 45, 218
Regret, 62, 64
Reid, T., 217
Religion, 117, 130–143
Remorse, 63, 64, 68
Renaissance, 20, 21, 212
Retaliation, 125, 126, 127
Rhabditis nigrovenosa, 113
Ritter, W. E., 17, 137, 220
Robertson, G. S., 126
Rogers, A. K., 215
Romanes, G. J., 83, 92
Romanes, Miss, 83
Roosevelt, T., 82
Ross, E. A., 196
Ross, W. D., 10, 11
Rousseau, J. J., 102
Royce, J., 33
Ruskin, J., on war, 195
Russell, B., 223
Ryan, J., 145

Sadism, 97
Sanger, M., 159, 223
Santayana, G., 11
Satan, 72, 211
Schelling, F. W. J., 217
Schiller, F. C. S., 11

INDEX

Schopenhauer, A., 217
Schuman, F. L., 191, 225
Schurman, J. G., 65–67, 217, 221
Scott, J. W., 217
Seeman, B., 119
Selby-Bigge, L. A., 215
Selection, 3, 51. *See also* natural selection and group selection
Self-realization, 33–35, 42
Seth, J., 31, 33, 218
Sexual selection, 80
Shaftesbury, A., 22, 45, 216
Shame, 31, 64, 65, 67, 75, 84–89
Shand, A. F., 78, 84, 102
Sharp, F. C., 218
Shyness, 87, 88, 122
Sidgwick, H., 14, 31, 215, 216, 218
Silver Shirts, 188
Simmel, G., 218
Smith, Adam, 22, 216
Smith, T. V., 218
Smith, W. H., 223
Sneath, E. H., 215
Social heredity, 55
Solitary wasps, 105
Sorley, W. R., 7, 9, 33, 34, 37, 222
Spencer, H., 1, 4, 34–38, 44, 58–60, 73, 94, 98, 101, 116, 131, 132, 176, 214, 219, 222, 223
Spinoza, B., 73
Standards of morals, 17–49, 144–162
Starbuck, E. D., 142, 143, 223
Steinmetz, S. R., 197, 224
Stephen, Leslie, 56, 85, 86, 216, 219
Stewart, D., 27, 45, 217
Stopes, M., 223
Stratton, G. M., ix, 82, 225
Sumner, W. G., 100, 116, 222, 223
Supernaturalism, 5, 7, 137–141, 151
Survival, 39, 46, 55, 71
Sutherland, A., 92, 93, 116, 128, 219, 222
Sutherland, H. G., 156, 161, 224
Sympathy, 31, 51, 52, 56, 57, 60–63, 65, 67, 69, 90–93, 129

Tarde, G., 91

Taureg, clan morals of, 123
Tawney, R. H., 189
Taylor, A. E., 9, 218
Ten Commandments, 18
Tender emotion, 93–95
Tertullian, 167–168 note
Theognis, 206
Third International, 182, 183
Thorndike, E. L., 221
Thurn, I., 127
Tolstoi, L., 193, 194
Torrey, H. B., ix
Trotter, W., 224
Tsanoff, R. A., 215
Tufts, J., 218
Tylor, E. B., 117, 130, 222, 223
Tyndall, J., 15

Ueberweg, F., 215
Urban, W. M., 218
Utilitarianism, 22–28, 40, 45, 46, 57

Veddahs, 123, 128
Veracity, 123, 181, 196
Vindictiveness, 127
Vis medicatrix naturae, 2, 185

Wagner, K., 199
Waitz, T., 127
Wake, E. S., 215
Wallace, A. R., 73, 110, 123
Wanika, 131
War, 81, 177–182, 188, 191–201, 211–213
Ward, H., 225
Ward, J., 9
Wasmann, E., 75
Welfare as moral standard, 35, 36, 45, 46, 48, 49
Westermarck, E., 41, 42, 45, 100, 116, 118, 119, 126, 130, 133, 214, 215, 219, 220, 222, 223
Whewell, Wm., 27, 217
White, F. W., 223
Wiggam, A. E., 225
Wilcox, W. F., 223
Williams, Cora M., 219
Wilson, Woodrow, 203

Windelband, W., 215
Wissler, C., 222
Witches, persecution of, 57, 100, 137–139
Wright, Q., 225
Wundt, W., 215, 218, 223

Yang, 72
Yerkes, A. W., 221
Yerkes, R. M., 109, 110, 221

Zell, T., 221
Zuckermann, S., 110, 221